Slender
IS THE
Thread

The title of this book is respectfully borrowed
from the late John Young Brown, Sr., a great trial lawyer
who promised to write a book of that title but never did.

Slender
IS THE
Thread

Tales from a
Country Law Office

HARRY M. CAUDILL

THE UNIVERSITY PRESS OF KENTUCKY

Scholarly publisher for the Commonwealth,
serving Bellarmine College, Berea College, Centre
College of Kentucky, Eastern Kentucky University,
The Filson Club, Georgetown College, Kentucky
Historical Society, Kentucky State University,
Morehead State University, Murray State University,
Northern Kentucky University, Transylvania University,
University of Kentucky, University of Louisville,
and Western Kentucky University.

Editorial and Sales Offices: Lexington, Kentucky 40506-0024

Library of Congress Cataloging-in-Publication Data
Caudill, Harry M., 1922-
  Slender is the thread.

  1. Law—Kentucky—Letcher County—Anecdotes,
facetiae, satire, etc. 2. Courts—Kentucky—Letcher
County—Anecdotes, facetiae, satire, etc. 3. Letcher
County (Ky.)—Social life and customs. I. Title.
K184.C38 1987   349.769′163   87-1983
ISBN 0-8131-1611-2   347.69163

To Dr. Otis Singletary,
former president of the University of Kentucky,
whose understanding of Kentucky's economic,
social, and political problems exceeded
his power to resolve them.

Contents

Preface

IN A SUPPLEMENT to his *The American Language* H.L. Mencken encapsulated the early history of Kentucky: "What is now Kentucky was the first region beyond the mountains to be settled. Pioneers began to invade it before the Revolution, and by 1782 it had more than 30,000 population. It was originally a part of Virginia, and the effort to organize it as an independent state took a great deal of politicking."

Implicit in these lines are the influences that gave the state and its people their reputation for contented ignorance, colorful individualism, crankiness, self-reliance, contempt for court decisions, deadliness with gun and knife, old-time salvation-style religion, and quirky and corrupt politics. In the decades since World War II new roads, television, and globalization of markets have caused a new Kentucky to emerge from the womb of time, but the old one, spawned of our British antecedents and the New World frontier, has not yet died. The new and old patterns of thought and behavior mingle in virtually every county and precinct, and give rise to such contradictions as our strange treatment of whiskey: our frontier era prompts us to make it, which we do in such immense quantities that it is known globally as bourbon after the county where it originated. But a religious revival, the Great Awakening, prompts us to reject it, so that three quarters of the counties—including Bourbon—are officially "dry" by vote of the people. As matters have evolved the whiskey pours from the stills, ministers deplore it from their pulpits, and most Kentuckians do their drinking at home. A split personality has a hard time making up its mind.

In my career as a lawyer I found the imprint of the Indian frontier everywhere. Notwithstanding the advent of soda pop, frozen TV dinners, and wayside fast-food joints, Kentuckians still relish the foods their ancestors ate in 1792—cornbread, pork, potatoes, and dried beans. Like those pioneers they still keep guns in their homes and close to hand. Nor have they lost the bonds of superstition. A thousand tales of "strange" occurrences are remembered, and few escape exhortations to repent. And when some governmental action is proposed, no matter how needed and benign, a roar of disapproval is heard as the frontier mind expresses its opposition to meddling by Jeffersonian "tyrants."

For not very good reasons Kentucky bills itself as the Bluegrass State. It could with more reason be styled the Pioneer State.

These stories were not recorded because the people in them were epic personalities or the events grandly dramatic. I have told them because they reflect the mighty story of poor European immigrants struggling on primitive land and in wild mountains to survive, reproduce, and find sustenance for themselves and their households. Little by little the forest receded, the streams were bridged, the wild animals retreated to waste lands and government-owned sanctuaries, the Indians moved to Oklahoma (but many left their genes behind), schools were opened and the light of knowledge began to flicker on the new farms and along muddy village streets. The struggle was incredibly hard. It is impossible for us air-conditioned moderns to comprehend the magnitude of the effort. Put another way, how many of our stellar university athletes could accompany a latter-day Andrew Jackson to New Orleans and back, in the heat, cold, and rain, mostly afoot and carrying an eleven-pound rifle? How well might they endure a ten-hour stint at a coal face shoveling the gleaming fuel into cars—and without any hope of escape until arthritis or a roof fall brings an end to their labors?

And in this easy age of scholarships and scholastic loans and grants, how can our tender youths comprehend schools without buses, lunchrooms, or libraries, and college educations paid for by small student wages earned over a decade or longer?

If some of these stories seem mindlessly violent, it is because the frontier experience attuned the people to weak governments, self-help, quick wrath, and long memories. The hundreds of volumes containing Kentucky court decisions are redolent of gunsmoke, red with blood, darkened with murder, lust, and vengeance. Jim Frazier and his son reflect the odiousness of crime and of a primitive social structure struggling to cope with it. And the horror of the Hillsville courthouse mirrors a culture and time when blood ties were the most valuable facets of life and any slight or burden, even when imposed by lawful courts, was ground for fiery resistance even to death. Nor should we suppose that the bloody age is behind us. A recent study disclosed that in eastern Kentucky eleven out of each thousand deaths are homicides, a rate that would horrify our British brethren.

Politics is a heady game in a simple society. Washington was elected to the Virginia House of Burgesses in a campaign in which he dispensed four-fifths of a gallon of spirits for each vote he received. The gallant who would become the father of his country wanted to win, and to win he had to "wet whistles," make promises, and pay off poll "floaters." This is not the way it should have been, but nonetheless the pattern was set and our elections remain in our time not only corrupt but subject to brutal pressures. Where Washington won votes by handing out whiskey and rum, the adroit politician of today may bestow not only whiskey and cash but public funds in the shape of welfare benefits, pensions, and wages, or even lift the burden of a prison sentence. The political machines are constantly building and dying as incumbents battle "reformers" who will, if elected, seek to repel others battering at their own walls. The emerging Kentucky has built magnificent roads and filled the heavens with the shouting of televised nonsense, but it has yet to inspire a majority of its people to want to learn, or to make its elections honest and fair.

These tales may help some to understand just how hard many Kentuckians have had to labor for their sustenance in trades

that consume lives as avidly as hungry Americans devour ham-
burgers. In Harlan County alone more than 1,365 coal miners
have died, most of them like the biblical sinner crushed between
upper and nether millstones. It is a precious price paid in
darkness and loneliness that our lights may continue to shine.
Like the Indian frontier faced by our ancestors, they daily
confront an industrial frontier of immeasurable terror and danger.

We go on and the stories about Kentucky accumulate. There
is no end of them. The people and their land remain picturesque,
violent, and challenging. And when Kentucky is as old as
France is now, the influences of what our forefathers did, and
what we do today, will still shape thoughts and inspire to action
people beyond our ken in the bottomless abyss of tomorrow. In
that sense the people in these stories are immortal. The lives of
such obscure common people are the building blocks and mortar
of history. If they appear to us hard, crude, and sometimes
brutal, we must concede in their defense that history forged
them in a cruel and turbulent furnace.

1. Country Lawyers

BEFORE THE Age of Television, Kentucky was a land of superlative storytellers. This trait was nurtured by the quixotic, individualistic, and introspective nature of the people—an ingrained quality spawned by a history that included Indian wars, prolonged rural isolation, a civil war fought at home, hardscrabble farming, oversize families, and, all too often, having to get by on not quite enough to go around. Under such circumstances many characters were created: fiercely independent people who cared scarcely at all about public opinion, did mainly as they pleased to the outrage of more conventional neighbors, and were prone to startling undertakings. Until a couple of decades ago the bar in almost every rural county possessed such people in full measure, and not a few presided as circuit judges. Their clients and their own experiences gave rise to marvelous tales. Federal Judge Mac Swinford caught the spirit of this now-vanished Kentuckian in his excellent little book *Kentucky Lawyer* (1963). I had the privilege of hearing from country lawyers innumerable stories of a kind that would have gladdened the heart of this distinguished jurist.

One such tale was recounted by Steve Combs, who practiced law at Whitesburg from 1912 to 1968 and thereafter was circuit judge for three years. In his long career he served for a time as United States commissioner, as a county judge, and as a soldier in World War I. Before he was a lawyer, he was a school teacher. In his old age he was "Judge Combs," but he always signed his name very formally as Stephen Combs, Jr. To an earlier generation, though, he was hailed as Little Steve to distinguish him from his locally-prominent uncle who, because of his towering height and ample girth, was Big Steve Combs. However he was addressed, he had a rich repertoire of colorful recollections and liked nothing so much as to relate one, especially at his home on a summer evening when a chilled watermelon had been brought under the knife.

On one such occasion, to illustrate a story he was about to tell, the judge quoted Shakespeare: "All the world's a stage and all the men and women merely players. They have their exits and their entrances and each man in his time plays many parts." With a bite of melon poised on his fork he described how he had once been dragooned into the role of a surgeon's assistant.

In 1912, when Steve was the newest lawyer at the Letcher County bar, Whitesburg was a primitive backwoods village. The tracks of the Louisville and Nashville Railroad arrived that year, pushing into the Elk Horn Coal deposits at the new town of Haymond. At Whitesburg the tracklayers found streets compounded of mud and generous quantities of horse manure. Such sidewalks as existed were made of wood, much of which had decayed or disappeared into the mire. Most homes were humble log structures that hid discreetly under an outer skin of white-painted drop siding. The practice of medicine was still largely in the calomel and quinine stage except for progressive, and therefore somewhat eccentric, Dr. P.Y. Pursifull, a youngish physician and surgeon who was much better educated than the country doctors who roamed the backlands making house calls. Dr. Pursifull was proficient in the general surgical techniques of the day and was a busy man with a promising future.

He had hung his shingle on a wooden building on a hill overlooking the town. The county's first hospital, it consisted of a waiting room with a dozen sturdy chairs, an examination room, and down the hall three or four rooms with beds where patients could be cared for after operations. The examination room contained a skylight for daytime illumination and hooks for lanterns. There was also a roll-top desk, a shelf or two of medical books, and a glass-cased display of surgical instruments. On other shelves were vials of medicines, bottles of isopropyl alcohol and hydrogen peroxide, stacks of clean sheets and towels, rubber gloves, and cans of ether. Elsewhere there was a small sink with a bucket of water and cake of soap for scrubs before operations. In the center of the room stood an operating table, about six and a half feet long and perhaps thirty inches wide, fashioned of wood by a local carpenter. On it was a thin mattress in a rubber container, covered by a white sheet. Here the doctor waged his struggle against the ills that flesh is heir to. For the time and the place it was an excellent facility.

At the end of one sunny Saturday, Steve Combs prepared to close his office. Such visitors as the county seat had seen that day had departed and the few merchants expected no more customers until Monday morning. But the day was not to end so quietly for Steve. He would remember the next two hours with complete clarity until his death seventy-three years later.

Dr. Pursifull suddenly appeared at the door of Steve's office. He was coatless and his sleeves were rolled up. "Thank God you are still here!" he declared. "You have got to help me out."

Pursifull explained that a man had been brought into town in a buggy over terrible creek roads and now lay groaning on the operating table. No other doctor was in town. The practical nurse who sometimes assisted him had gone home and could not be found. Steve was the only person within reach who could be of any assistance, and the patient desperately needed help. Mountain people referred to his ailment as cramp colic, but the doctor knew he had a pus-filled appendix that would soon burst. If that happened, death would follow from peritonitis. Time was running out and Steve was needed to administer ether! Steve pointed out that he did not know how to provide an anesthetic to a surgical patient, but the doctor said he would show him how. "All you have to do is pour ether on a pad and hold it over his nose till he passes out. Then do it again from time to time so he won't come to. I'll tell you when you need to give him another dose. They always begin to get restless when the ether starts to wear off!"

Then, fixing Steve with an unflinching gaze, he delivered the clincher: "So, you see, if you don't help me, I can't operate and if I can't operate, he will die—and it will all be your fault!"

The lawyer felt himself propelled along the muddy streets, then up the path to the surgery. There the patient's sons and wife hovered over him as he lay on his back moaning softly, his face flushed with morphine and fever.

The men and their mother were put out of the room and the door was shut after them. The doctor removed the patient's clothing, a process that brought piteous moans. Pursifull then thoroughly washed his hands, poured alcohol over them, and when they were dry, put on rubber gloves. Steve washed his own hands in the same manner and applied the alcohol. When he looked at the portly white form of the naked patient, he was reminded of the carcass of a freshly-slaughtered and scraped hog.

Steve took up the indicated cotton and gauze pad, slopped ether over it as admonished by the surgeon, and clamped it over the upturned nostrils. Within seconds the moaning stopped and the patient slept. Fortunately the windows were open for ventilation or Steve might have slept, too. Without further ado Pursifull made a longish slit where the appendix was supposed to be and, to Steve's horror and dismay, a length of intestine welled up and surged outward. Pursifull grumped, "He has had a lot to eat and his gut is full of gas." (Steve internally vowed to eat lightly thereafter.) There was no sign, however, of the appendix. "That's strange; it isn't here," growled the puzzled surgeon.

Steve swayed, his eyes bulging, as the scalpel flashed again. The incision grew to a startling length, weaving its way along an expanse of belly that looked as big as Texas. Each newly-exposed segment of bowel was eagerly examined, but the appendix did not reveal itself. Presently the patient stirred uneasily. Beads of sweat hanging from the end of his nose, the doctor commanded, "More ether!"

Pursifull was dumbfounded. How could a man have appendicitis if he had no appendix? Finally he said, "Keep him full of ether. I have got to take his guts out until I find that appendix, no matter how long it takes!"

The transfixed lawyer watched with open mouth and bulging eyes as fold upon fold of intestine were pulled "hand over hand like a butcher would pull strings of sausages out of a meat case." The white loops flecked with blood lay on the patient's abdomen, between his legs, and on his private parts. Steve was sicker than he had ever been in his life or would be again. The ether can was emptied and another was brought from the shelf. "Doc Pursifull was so busy hunting that appendix that he left the ether up to me and I gave him what I thought he ought to have," he chuckled.

Suddenly the doctor emitted a squeak of satisfaction. The misplaced appendix had turned up at last. Pursifull applied a clamp to it, snipped it off, and threw it into a bucket. Through the haze of his waking nightmare Steve saw it strike the bottom of the pail and exude yellow pus. At this point, he remembered, "I was in worse shape than the patient."

The clamped stub of the appendix was sewed up in what Steve recalled to be a workmanlike manner. The body cavity was swabbed out and washed with hydrogen peroxide. Then the surgeon began putting the intestine back where it belonged. When this process had continued for what seemed an eternity, another horror confronted the doctor and his unwilling assistant: the space that had contained the gut for fifty years was no longer big enough. While outside the cavity, the bowel had become distended. On the brink of tears, Steve had a strong impulse to just sit down and cry.

Pursifull paused for a moment, then the scalpel flashed anew, extending the incision to a most marvelous length. Fingers stuffed in more segments of gut but, alas, the elusive organ welled up elsewhere. Steve was commanded to help and felt the bloated tube-like organ squishing in his sweaty fingers. With a mighty effort, he and the doctor finally got it all inside. Then Pursifull pushed from one direction and Steve shoved from the other to bring together the unwilling sides of the abdomen. Fortunately the gargantuan applications of ether kept the patient tranquil as Pursifull applied first clamps, then cat-gut sutures. Steve leaned over the body straining with a hand on each side of the vast incision, his perspiration dropping onto the bloody flesh, his arms and legs feeling as heavy as stone. His gloved hands working steadily, the doctor occasionally hummed a few bars from some popular song. When the last suture was in place, the large, traumatized belly was washed and dried, then bandaged. Steve thought the bandage would have upholstered at least a chair.

At last the work was over except for cleaning up. Pursifull

grabbed a mop and shoved it over the bloody floor. The soiled sheet was removed from under the sufferer and a clean one inserted. Another sheet was spread over the now-sighing patient. The operation was over.

Steve looked at himself in a wall mirror. Pursifull's surgical apron had kept his clothes clean, but Steve was a ruin. His shirt front was as bloody as if he had been shot. Blood splotched his trousers and shoes. His hair was limp with sweat. His eyes were bloodshot, his face haggard. The surgeon was generous in his expressions of gratitude. Steve staggered wearily away to his room in a boarding house. That night he experienced a series of nightmares and was so tired the next morning that he stayed in bed all day.

The patient's sons carried him to a room where he could be looked after and begin the slow process of healing. Steve went daily to visit him, sometimes with Pursifull. In time, he recovered and went home.

Months later when Steve encountered him on the street, he asked the usual "Well, how are you today?" The heartfelt reply came, "To tell you the truth, Steve, I still have a mighty sore belly!"

Another native of Letcher County, J.L. Hays, told me about his one and only venture into preaching the gospel. A feisty contemporary of Judge Combs, Hays arrived at the county seat bar in the late autumn of 1922 fresh from the University of Kentucky law college. Unlike Steve Combs, who was bone dry, Hays liked his nip of Kentucky bourbon and generally kept a bottle of it within easy reach. During the dark days of Prohibition, he and his law partner, Doug Day, preserved outdated volumes of the Kentucky Statutes. The pages of these huge, thick tomes were cut with razor blades to form close-fitting receptacles for pint bottles. Sometimes an entire row of these impressive-looking books provided refreshment to moist, wet, or wringing wet Kentucky lawyers. For that generation of rural barristers a convivial glass with fellow counselors, amenable judges, friends and clients was more or less customary at the end of the working day, and the hollow books were frequently refilled. During Prohibition the dependable straight corn of moonshiners was relied upon, but after repeal mellow bourbon returned to its place of esteem.

Between 1922 and his death in 1968 Hays served a term as commonwealth attorney, two terms as county attorney, and eight years as circuit judge of the 47th Kentucky Circuit. On the bench the phrasing of his rulings was sometimes unorthodox. Once a lawyer asked leave to approach the bench, whereupon he vigorously argued for permission to show the jurors a pre-viously-excluded document. A brisk discussion ensued in whis-pers that grew increasingly loud. Finally the judge slammed down his gavel and shouted, "Damn it to hell, you can't do that!"

On one occasion before he became circuit judge, I asked him what the initials J.L. stood for and he replied testily, "Not a damn thing!" It seems that he was named for his mother's brother who was known simply as "L" (pronounced Ell). This letter stood for a name which had fallen into total disuse when the uncle was a child and was wholly forgotten when L.'s parent died. Thus the future judge began life with an initial but no name. He said that one initial was not enough so he adopted another to go with it.

Hays was small, quick-tempered, and, before time thinned and whitened his locks, red-haired. He was so utterly Irish in appearance that he would have seemed perfectly at home on the streets or in the pubs of Dublin. He was an excellent stump speaker, quick in repartee, and a keen student of the law. He was thoroughly honest in every respect. He did, as I have said, like his nip, and his being called to preach grew out of this.

One Saturday night in 1922, his senior year at law school, he and a friend got drunk. The fellow imbiber was not a law student with a leisurely day before him to sleep off the ill effects of too much alcohol. A senior at the Lexington Theological Seminary, then on the campus of Transylvania College, the lad would soon graduate, be ordained, and assume the cloth of a Methodist minister. But like father Noah who became drunk on wine, the budding minister was not above sin, especially where spirits and lissom girls were concerned.

The preacher-to-be was awakened on Sunday by the light of a crisp spring morning spreading over the Kentucky bluegrass. His head felt mightily enlarged and throbbed as if a steam

engine were at work between his temples. All his limbs were
heavy and unresponsive. He pulled a pillow over his head to
return to sleep but was suddenly galvanized by a remembered
duty. It was 7:30 and he had agreed to appear at a country
church in an adjoining county at 10:45. The small congregation
had long been without a pastor and had sought the services of a
student minister. The seminary dean who handled such matters
had discussed it with L.'s friend, pointing out that this was an
opportunity to acquire valuable experience that could lead to a
pastoral call. The brash young theologian had accepted with
relish and informed the church's governing board of his intent to
arrive by the interurban electric railroad that then connected
Lexington with numerous county seats.

He studiously applied himself to organizing a sermon, which
he outlined on note cards. His best blue suit and white shirt
were made ready, his black shoes were neatly polished and laid
by. Every essential preparation had been made in advance and
he had looked forward to carrying the word to this hungry flock.
But now all was lost. His pain-racked body made the expedition
impossible. Even if he could drag himself to the church, he
would be unable to perform. When he staggered out of bed and
looked at his note cards, the misery in his head intensified.
When he glanced at a mirror, the eyes he beheld were bloodshot
and yellow-gray bags hung beneath them. The hopelessness of
his position was complete. Then a light broke in upon him like a
sun's ray that penetrates to the mossy floor of a dense forest.

Across the then little city of Lexington there was a knock on
the door of L.'s dormitory room. He was summoned to the public
telephone in the hall. The sad, distraught, wheedling voice of his
drinking buddy poured out the tale of woe. With sighs and
lamentations the predicament was outlined. Then, with a
prayerful entreaty a solution was proposed. The law student
should assume the duties the theological student could not
perform. L., it was pointed out, had suffered no ill effects from
the binge. He could take his friend's Bible and sermon notes and
study them on the interurban train. He could fill most of the
time with songs and by calling on one prominent brother, and
then another, to pray. He would need to preach for no more than
twenty minutes, and not much of a sermon would be expected of

a mere student preacher. L. could bring it off without a doubt. The alternatives were spelled out: a missed appointment, an investigation, expulsion from the seminary, disgrace and infamy at home and elsewhere. Then a piteous, wailing plea: "Please L., for God's sake, don't let me down!"

"They'll know damned well I'm not you. If I go over there impersonating a Methodist preacher, we'll both get expelled," roared a dubious L.

Still, the prospect appealed to him. The whole affair had been arranged by mail and telephone, so no one at the church had met the guest minister. They knew only his name, approximate age, and that he was white. L. would qualify in all these respects. The ham actor in him yearned for expression. It was the same quality that would later make him an effective trial lawyer. With minimal reluctance but many protests, he agreed to attempt to preserve his friend's career.

He showered, shampooed, and shaved. The shirt he put on was white, the cravat dark wine. His blue suit carried a knife-edge crease and his shoes were freshly buffed. A few minutes on the streetcar took him to his suffering friend.

The Bible that was put in his hand was paper-clipped to indicate the text. "Watch and pray, that ye enter not into temptation: the spirit indeed is willing, but the flesh is weak." On a half-dozen crisp cards were notes and quotations to elucidate the scriptural passage. Another card contained the names and callings of the leading figures in the church. The now-hopeful theologian promised that he would never forget this noble act.

The sunlight beamed on the bluegrass as the little electric cars hurtled along. The law student pondered the biblical text and the circumstances in which it was voiced by Jesus. He considered the note cards but found them of little interest. His father was a "stem-winding" mountain lawyer and L. had grown to manhood listening to his impromptu speeches in courtrooms and on political stumps. He had no intention of preaching from some other person's ideas.

When he left the car, he walked a few hundred yards along an asphalted lane to a neat little steepled church. Behind it were the discreet grave markers of departed believers. The surprisingly large crowd that had gathered greeted him with smiles and handshakes. The fraudulent young shepherd introduced himself and received approving nods from men and women who appraised him with honest, level stares. There were, also, shapely young women, at least one of whom he had seen on the University of Kentucky campus. Amid pleasant remarks he went inside the church. A sturdy yeoman tugged at a rope and a bell clanged to urge latecomers to hasten.

L. had attended a similar church at Whitesburg and knew the general routine of such worship services. Promptly at 11:00 he nodded to the middle-aged woman seated at the piano, which was more or less in tune. In his recollection of the episode forty years later, "She promptly played a doleful tune that got the crowd into a solemn mood."

L. was seated on the dais with a couple of elders who passed the collection plates, ushered, and generally revelled in making announcements. When the music had run its course, the young minister stood up, looked steadfastly at the upturned faces and stepped to the pulpit. He had the audience under control and, like a skilled lawyer working a jury, was determined to retain his dominance. His eyes went along the rows of wooden benches, touching for a fragment of a second each pair of eyes. Then, his hands on the podium, he intoned, "Let us praise God for his mercies!"

He began in a low voice that rose and sank in the melodramatic style he had heard in country courtrooms. He fervently thanked God for a wide range of benefits: the earth and the fullness thereof; this wonderful day with its sparkling sunlight; the great gift of life and the kind and loving parents through whom it came; this worshipful congregation; the young and pious sons and daughters; health; and, most emphatically of all, the promise of eternal life, and the Blessed Savior who had died a dreadful death on a gruesome cross to open the gates of heaven to repentant sinners. When at last he paused and said, "Amen," there were several seconds of complete silence before the bowed heads were raised in solemn expectation.

By way of general introduction he told them his name—the assumed name, of course, of his unhappy friend. He thanked them for this opportunity to stand before this "consecrated congregation in this House of God." He asked God to bless "all that we undertake here today."

He opened a hymnal with such a brisk flourish that it popped like a hand clap. The old tattered book had warmed the hearts of the congregation for generations, and he called their attention to a song easy to sing, admonishing them to sing with all their "strength and power":

> O God, our strength, to thee our song
> with grateful hearts we raise;
>
> To thee, and thee alone, belong
> all worship, love and praise.

As the verses progressed, the response from the congregation grew. When they had finished, he beamed and said, "Let's do it again! I love whole-soul people and let's sing it with whole souls and no holding back!"

The volume of sound increased to a roar, the preacher singing at the top of his lungs. Then he turned to "There is a Fountain Filled with Blood" and had the men and boys sing it while the women and girls were quiet. Then he silenced the men and boys and turned the women and girls loose. Faces reddened with enjoyment and exertion as he let the adults sing in competition against the young people, then "all together for the Lord." They got going in high gear on "Angels from the Land of Glory," ordinarily a Christmas song but tailor-made for the occasion and the mood. When the enthusiastic worshipers had settled into their pews, he sent forth two dignified brothers with the collection plates. A brief prayer sanctified the coins and bills when they were safely at rest in the hands of the treasurer.

L. then opened the great pulpit Bible and read from St. Matthew 26:41. Intoxicated by his rapport with the crowd he gave them what they wanted—"old time hell-fire and damnation." They were hungry for the unvarnished word. He asked rhetorically, "Why is spiritual rebirth necessary?" and answered with, "To make a sinner simple and trusting like a child." And why should one become childlike instead of wise like a sage? "Because," he thundered, "God will not condemn the trusting child, but woe unto the man who is filled with worldly wisdom and stumbles to damnation!" He gave them entire lines from Bunyan's *The Pilgrim's Progress* and bade them look inward to the burdens they were bearing. He admonished them to ask themselves, "Am I walking with the Pilgrim to the City of God, or am I slinking with Mr. Worldly Wiseman to Perdition?" Then, "There is a hot and burning hell. Each of us knows the path he is on and He knows, too [pointing upward], that at the end of our journeys each must stand naked and alone before the judgment seat of God!"

Here there were sobs and sighs. The preacher stepped back and called on a dignified elderly gentleman (identified on one of the cards as a wealthy farmer and businessman) to dismiss the service with a prayer. The good man responded at length. He thanked the Lord for many things, and most particularly "for this blessed young man who has come into our midst and lifted up our spirits in such a wondrous way."

When the crowd was outside, a dozen dinner invitations came thick and fast, all heartfelt, generous, and sincere. But the old gentleman of the dismissal prayer was not to be denied and bore the preacher away on the front seat of his Dodge touring car, while from the back seat his wife and daughter poured out their fervent approval of the service.

That evening the much-restored friend heard L.'s report. He was full of praise for L.'s performance and was generous with his expression of gratitude. His spirits were high as he contemplated the successful ruse that had saved him from disaster.

All went well with the two young mountebanks until the morning of the following Saturday. On that otherwise beautiful day, L. was summoned to the telephone to hear the seminarian pour out the new troubles now threatening his ruin.

"L., I am destroyed!" he began. "You went over there and preached such a good sermon that they want me to come back tomorrow, and permanently after that. They have arranged to pay me a hundred and fifty dollars a month and fix up the manse for me. A delegation is with the president now, and he has sent for me to come to his office. It is a grand proposition, and I can't accept it. I can't even go and meet them. Don't you see what you have done? It is you they want, not me!" Then after a hysterical gasp, "What on earth are we going to do?"

This brought L.'s Irish blood to a boil. "I'm not going to do a damn thing!" he shouted. "I'm through with preaching. You can call the president and make any excuse you want to. Tell him you will not come to his office, and that you will not meet with the delegation, and that you will not go back there to preach under any circumstance whatever! Put your foot down on the matter. They will all be as mystified as hell, but they will get over it." Then he added, "You had better run and hide out for a while or they will put two and two together for certain!" He hung up amid wails from the other end of the wire.

Consternation, mystification, chagrin, and injured feelings settled in high places at the seminary and in the little country church. The president of the seminary branded the student's behavior beastly, ungracious, and ungentlemanly, and told him so as soon as he could find him. He demanded an explanation and that the student apologize to the church in person, but L.'s friend remained as adamant as a stone post. He would not explain his reasons for such offensive behavior, and said not even a team of horses could drag him back to that congregation, even for a single moment. The episode caused much head wagging, and many frowns and sighs.

As to what happened later, L. said the friendship came to a shattering halt. "He got mad at me," the judge grumped. "He claimed that I got him into the worst mess of his life."

Another memorable practitioner at the Letcher County bar in the days of my youth was tall, courteous John D.W. Collins. I never learned what the initials stood for and John may have forgotten, for sometimes, when he was in an exuberant mood, he would sign pleadings and letters with a resounding "John D.W.X.Y.Z. Collins." John was probably the happiest individual I have ever known. In good times and bad, in victory and defeat, he invariably saw the humor in a situation and laughed with his characteristic "tee-hee."

John was born about 1880 and, like hundreds of other mountaineers, walked out of the hills to Lexington to volunteer for the

Spanish-American war. The trip took five days of trudging along creek paths and through hill gaps. After hurried training John was armed with an 1871 model single-shot, black-powder rifle and sent to Cuba to fight Spaniards who carried modern, magazine-loading, high-powered German Mausers. John said it was a good thing that the army equipped its soldiers with big hats "because after each shot we had to fan away the powder smoke to see whether we had hit anything. Tee-hee!"

When John came home, he read law and was admitted to the bar. He practiced at least forty years and his unrestrainable "tee-hee" broke the gravity of every imaginable kind of court proceeding from divorce hearings to argument in murder cases.

In 1936 Troy Triplett was tried in Letcher Circuit Court for murder and John defended him. The case was notorious and the facts were atrocious. John did his best, of course, as did the commonwealth attorney. The courtroom was jammed to overflowing when the jury returned after deliberating a full ten minutes. A silence like the soundlessness of a cavern passed over the crowd. Necks craned so eyes could see, and breathing stopped as the clerk accepted the verdict sheet. Judge Monroe Fields intoned the usual question, "Gentlemen of the jury, have you reached a verdict?" and the foreman replied in a low, emotional voice, "We have your honor." The judge then directed the clerk to read the verdict.

A veteran court clerk invariably makes the most of such a moment, and this occasion was used to the utmost. The clerk removed his glasses and polished them thoroughly with a handkerchief. He then refolded the handkerchief and restored it to his pocket. The cleaned spectacles were returned to his nose, then adjusted and readjusted to secure a proper fitting. The verdict was unfolded and studied as suspense gripped the audience. The clerk's eyes went round the courtroom from wall to wall and along row after row of seats. He cleared his throat while hundreds of hearts pounded in hundreds of chests. Then came, "We, the jury, do find the defendant guilty as charged. . . ." This much had been universally expected, but what of the penalty? Would it be life imprisonment or the chair? Now the silence deepened even more and every person in the courtroom was frozen to complete immobility as the clerk paused, reexamined the sheet of paper, repositioned his eyeglasses firmly on his nose, glanced again at the packed courtroom, cleared his throat anew and resumed, "and fix his punishment [another excruciating pause] at death in the electric chair!"

After this performance the stillness remained absolute as eyes shifted to the defendant and his lawyer. How would Triplett react to this pronouncement of doom? What would his attorney do in so dramatic and painful a situation? The two men's eyes met for a long moment. Then John smiled and clapped Triplett on the shoulder with his huge, Lincolnesque hand. "Well, Troy," he said, "there is one good thing about it. They can't electrocute your lawyer! Tee hee."

In his old age John had to live in a veterans hospital. Emmett Fields, a commonwealth attorney who appreciated the old gentleman's esteem for Kentucky bourbon, visited and left him a pint of Old Fitzgerald. John consumed it with intemperate haste and, like Omar Khayyam, became "drunken and of a merry mind." This kindled the wrath of his physician, who demanded to know the name of the culprit who had provided the liquor. John replied that it was a Russian secret agent. "The Russians," he explained, "will do absolutely anything to get a Spanish-American war veteran drunk. Tee-hee." When pressed for details, he said that he had gotten so old he could no longer remember names, faces, dates, or places. Tee-hee.

In 1922 John became involved in the Noble Crusade. The abuse of alcohol had become so pervasive and its ill effects so ruinous that a prohibition amendment to the United States Constitution had been approved by Congress and ratified by the states. Federal and state statutes imposed severe penalties for making, possessing, transporting, selling, or giving away any "spirituous, vinous or malt liquors," and a determined campaign was underway to break the American people of the liquor habit. Since its first settlement Kentucky had been a major producer of alcoholic beverages, and knowledge of whisky distilling was widespread. Throughout the hill country hardy entrepreneurs resolved to make their fortunes while the drought prevailed. Other mountaineers were employed by the government to enforce the prohibition act, and the result was a mighty and perpetual hubbub in the hills and mountains east of Mount

Sterling. Among these redoubtable enforcement officers were Sam Collins, of Whitesburg, Federal Prohibition Director for Kentucky, and his cousin, John D.W. The latter was one of many war veterans who were enticed away from farms, law offices, and stores by the lure of dependable salaries in a federal agency.

About 1960 Sam Collins told me about the years of strife engendered by prohibition, a strife so persistent and deadly as to border on overt insurrection. He described, too, one of the bloodiest episodes of the era and perhaps the boldest challenge to federal authority in Kentucky since the Civil War. Lighting up a fresh cigar he smiled whimsically at the memory of the dinner John D.W. served on Slate Creek in Menifee County at the end of the "Bob Ballard war."

It seems that prohibition agents in Cincinnati discovered a massive flow of moonshine whiskey to the city's speakeasies and other underworld establishments. Some was being moved by trainmen in boxcars returning empty from coal-field wholesales and commissaries, and the rest was carried by blockade runners in cars and trucks. Further undercover work led to the farm of Jeff Ballard where his sons Jeff and Bob and a number of their confederates were moonshining on a wholesale scale. The two brothers were reported to be extremely courageous, very dangerous, and crack shots with their Winchester rifles and .45 revolvers. They were not men who could be bluffed and any effort to end their operation would be risky work for brave men.

On December 9, 1922, six men led by prohibition agent Bob Duff raided the operations. On the way they met and captured Jeff Ballard and left him behind as a prisoner guarded by Duff's son. When they reached the still, they found a sturdy log fort defended by two skilled marksmen, Bob and Charlie Ballard. They attacked the fort and in the ensuing gunfire agent Duff was riddled with sixteen bullets. The United States retreated. When the agents returned in the afternoon, the Ballards had disappeared. Duff's body had been stripped of all valuables, including watch, pistol, badge, and money.

The next day the raiding party, twenty strong, was led by a United States commissioner. John D.W. was in that party and helped destroy a huge still and pour out a thousand gallons of mash and fifty gallons of moonshine. They had found the place deserted and commenced a search for the stillers on the surrounding hills. They were armed with Browning automatic and Krag-Jorgenson military rifles. John had one of the latter and a bandoleer filled with .30-calibre, armor-piercing cartridges. Though they were skilled woodsmen and hunters, they found none of the Ballards. The Ballards were about, however, for suddenly a bullet from the pinnacle of a distant cliff killed agent David Treadway.

With two agents dead, matters had become very serious. Sam Collins announced that "every effort will be made until the fugitives have been brought to justice." The use of bombing planes was considered and overruled, in part because only the year before six of the Air Force's antiquated DH-4s had crashed while flying from Washington to the battleground of the "Mingo County war" in West Virginia.

The Ballard war was quiet for a few days, but resumed on December 15 when twenty men, including John D.W., arrived early in the morning at the embattled Ballard farm. As they advanced up Slate Creek, all men encountered at the houses were summarily handcuffed to trees to prevent them from joining or warning the people at the Ballard fort. Anyone who joined the Ballards would be shot was the warning. This time Agent Guy Cole was killed by a .45-revolver bullet. Charlie Ballard jumped out a window amid a hail of shots and fled around a hillside. He ran a zig-zag course, returning fire all the while, and, though wounded, made his way to a waiting horse and escaped. He managed to get to Bath County, where he was arrested a few days later. He had been shot in the calf of each leg and in his shoulder.

Bob Ballard was not so fortunate. The federal and state officers offered no quarter and he asked for none. The Brownings blurted out fifteen rounds at a clip and the magazines were emptied time and again into the walls, roof, doors, and windows of the old hewed-log house. Chips flew from the roof and walls and there was the incessant ping of ricochets.

When a cease-fire was ordered, the bolted door was battered down and officers rushed in with drawn pistols. John was among the first to enter the shattered building. Bob Ballard lay on the floor unconscious. Bullets had passed through his head, a shoulder, both hips, an arm, and a leg. By each hand lay a .45 pistol. Nearby were three Winchester rifles and cases of cartridges. Incredibly, Ballard was not dead. With bloody lips and deep gasps he continued breathing for an hour.

In the Kentucky hills there are occasional "chimney cliffs," ledges of rock that can be pried out and lifted up in smooth slabs about two inches thick. These were customarily cemented together to form chimneys. Bob Ballard had used such slabs as part of the architecture of his fort. Inside his log walls he had erected inch-thick oak ceiling boards about two or three inches back from the logs. Into this space between logs and ceiling were inserted slabs of the stone. Even armor-piercing bullets zinged away when they struck such a barrier.

The men were hungry and tired after their long horseback ride and the excitement of the battle. There was a fire smoldering in Ballard's iron step-stove. Beans had been cooked and set aside. There was a huge pan of warm cornbread and a skillet full of fried sidemeat. An ancient coffee pot was full of hot brew. John found a plate and cup amid the debris in a cupboard and appeared with a full plate in one hand and an invigorating cup of coffee in the other. "Dinner's ready boys. Eat all you want as long as it lasts, compliments of Bob Ballard!"

He sat down by his unconscious host in a homemade chair and began to shovel in the country grub. Officer Creed Bentley of Pikeville shook his head ruefully. "I don't see how you can sit down and eat a man's dinner, John, while he is dying within a foot of your chair," he demurred.

But John chewed another mouthful of beans and bacon, then savored the coffee. Looking down at the expiring Ballard he allowed, "There's no use to let it waste after he cooked it. Besides, where he is going he would rather have a glass of ice water! Tee-hee."

Harry L. Moore was another Letcher County lawyer from whom I learned much. He grew up in New York not far from the Hyde Park country estate of James Roosevelt. When young Franklin Delano became lonesome for playmates, his mother would send the coach and driver out to collect willing children. Harry was always glad to go because Mrs. Roosevelt invariably served ice cream and cake to the urchins. The future president was "very bossy" even as a child, Harry said, and always wanted to "run everything to suit himself."

In time Harry grew up and made his way through law school. The Roosevelts and their Delano relatives had extensive stock holdings in coal companies, including Consolidation Coal, the largest of them all. Early in this century "Consol" built two huge new mining towns, Jenkins and McRoberts, in Letcher County and one of the Roosevelts kindly suggested to the new counsellor that he seek his fortune amid the vast coal boom that was underway in the Kentucky hills. He came south to check on the situation and stayed. Jenkins eventually reached a population of nearly 11,000 and was fitted out with every essential, including a city hall and police station. The coal company owned everything in the place "hell deep and heaven high"—each house, sidewalk, road gravel, and blade of grass. The turbulent new metropolis had to be governed firmly and fairly, and in accordance with company policies, so two budding young lawyers were promptly installed in important positions. Harry L. became the first city attorney and none other than John D.W. Collins was sworn in as its first police judge.

In those days municipal elections were unknown in mining towns. Under Kentucky law, to be eligible for a city office one had to live within the city limits, and that required the company's consent and approval. A person without approval was considered a trespasser and was subject to arrest. If a resident was elected without company approval or after an election pursued policies the company did not like, he could be compelled to leave the premises. This action vacated the office, which would then be filled by appointment of the county judge pursuant to the company's recommendation. Consequently, no one ran for mayor, alderman, or any other position. In an election year a list of recommended persons was taken to the county courthouse some time before January 1. These people were appointed by the judge. Good order was thus preserved, the cost and commotion of local elections were avoided, and, in the opinion of the coal magnates, the best men ruled over the destinies of the municipality and its free-born citizens. In this manner Harry L. and John D.W. came to occupy adjoining offices in the new, red-brick city hall. John explained to me that this left the people of Jenkins perfectly free—"perfectly free to mine coal. Tee-hee."

John described the rise and fall of George Fugate, for many years now a resident of Lexington and a great storyteller in his own right. It seems that George returned from World War I as a brash young lieutenant and was employed by Consolidation Coal as a bookkeeper. He and some other young veterans waited until the fifty-ninth minute of the eleventh hour appointed for such purpose and presented themselves at the county court clerk's office where they filed as candidates for mayor and members of the city council. Since no one else had filed, they were automatically certified as elected. George was proud to be mayor of so enterprising a town, but, alas, his elation was short-lived. The general manager explained to him the political facts of life in Jenkins, Kentucky. He concluded with, "Now, George, if you fellows don't resign, you will be fired and then you won't have jobs or offices either. The company cannot have just anyone running for office in the town." The upshot was that they promptly resigned and the county judge appointed dependable people to succeed them. "They just didn't understand company policy," John tee-heed.

Discussing the corporate rule at places like Jenkins, John D.W. declared that "everything was company! It was a company town with company houses, company streets, and company stores. The miners were company employees and, when they died, they were buried in a company cemetery. Harry was the company city attorney and I was the company judge. Herman Lee Donovan—later president of the University of Kentucky— was the company school superintendent. If anybody got out of line, he was put in the company jail. People even went to a company church and listened to a company preacher." Then with one of his irrepressible twinkles and a vintage tee-hee, he said, "The Big Shots even prayed to a company God, and died and went to a company heaven."

Another interesting personality among the Whitesburg lawyers bore the unlikely name of French Hawk. He was a farmer's son and grew up near Johnson City, Tennessee. In his youth he took a turn at professional baseball, then forsook the diamond for the courtroom. In 1917 when he got his law degree, he loaded all his possessions in two suitcases and headed for the turmoil and litigation that seethed in Letcher County, Kentucky. He arrived at the county seat with the two suitcases and seven dollars. And, though he became a man of considerable wealth, he always insisted that he was "too poor to leave." He habitually worked "six days a week and an hour or two on Sunday." He was a skilled trial lawyer whose eyes flashed like lightning while his voice boomed like thunder. He loved trials. If a client was too poor to pay him, he would often take the case anyway "just for the hell of it."

About 1935 French wrecked his Buick in an accident that rammed his head against the windshield. The collision left deep indentations and scars which he attempted to conceal by wearing a hat which only the most urgent necessity could compel him to remove. Judges generally indulged him in this idiosyncrasy. The spectacle of his huge, stoop-shouldered form, his big hands gesticulating and deep voice booming, his gray felt hat securely in place and pulled down close above his shaggy brows, was one that trial jurors never forgot. After one of Mr. Hawk's clients had been acquitted, the prosecuting attorney grumped that "French scared the jury into turning him loose."

Harry Moore told me how the auto accident led to a remarkable adventure in 1937 after French had replaced the wrecked car with an even larger, "top of the line" Buick. It was long and coal black, with a vast straight-eight engine and no end of power. French rubbed it down regularly with a chamois cloth so its coat would remain glossy. It was the apple of his eye and rested each night safe and secure in a tightly-locked garage.

One spring day in 1937 an event happened which involved several lawyers in a most vexatious case and brought French Hawk and his Buick to grief. Without a whisper of warning a thick slab of slate fell from the roof of the McRoberts mine and killed a black coal miner. He was without relatives in Letcher County and he was buried in a cheap coffin in an ill-kept hillside "nigger graveyard." His dependents were entitled to receive workmen's compensation benefits, but none of his fellow workmen knew anything about his origins or relatives. In addition, he owned a five thousand dollar life insurance policy which he had bought through a joint plan Consolidation Coal Company offered its employees. The named beneficiary was his estate. Alltold a neat sum of money was available for someone—about $20,000 in a depression year when thirty dollars a week was a high wage for an industrial worker.

The company called the matter to the attention of the county judge, who appointed French administrator of the dead man's estate. French rummaged through the miner's meager possessions, which had been preserved in a cardboard box by the manager of a company boarding house. There were scuffed shoes with soles worn thin, a cheap pocket watch, a few dollars in a frayed wallet, and some shirts, trousers, and socks. The identification card in the wallet contained the name James Wright and the simple address McRoberts, Kentucky. The thing French was looking for was found in the only additional item, a dirty, dog-eared copy of *Up from Slavery* by Booker T. Washington. The price noted on the frontispiece was forty-nine cents. There was a scarcely literate penciled presentation note from "Moma, Mary Wright." By a most happy turn of fortune she had included her address. She lived on a cotton plantation in southern Georgia and wrote that she loved her boy.

This discovery led to others that spun a tangled web indeed. It demonstrated that where there is money to be had, there spring up inventive minds and eager hands to claim it. French wrote Moma to inform her of the death of her son and to inquire whether he had been married and had children. Back came another penciled scrawl to express her grief and to say that she was James Wright's only dependent, that he had regularly sent support money, and that he was unmarried and childless. If this was true, Moma was clearly entitled to all the money.

But subsequent developments placed this uncomplicated statement in most serious doubt. It also unfolded a classic example of the Old South before the Great Society, the civil rights movement, the federal voting rights act, the outlawing of Jim Crow, the integrating of schools, the electing of black public officials, the industrializing of the sun belt, and the vast migration of black people from the cotton rows to the cities.

French immediately received sworn applications for the

money to be paid to Mary Wright, the decedent's mother. This document was forwarded to him by a Georgia lawyer. Shortly afterwards, other Georgia counselors contacted J.L. Hays and Harry Moore with similar applications, each signed Rosa Wright, the purported common-law wife of James Wright and mother of his child. A few days later another Georgia lawyer forwarded papers signed and verified by a *third* Rosa Wright. In the meantime, the insurers had paid French the money for which they were liable and he faced the task of deciding which of the wives was the proper claimant, and to what extent the mother should be compensated.

French arranged for a hearing to be held before a commissioner in the Georgia county seat at which the four claimants and their respective counsel could appear. There and then, under oath, they and their witnesses could undertake to prove the bona fides of their claims. Obviously the administrator, and ultimately a Kentucky judge, would need Solomonic wisdom if justice was to be done.

Thus it came to pass that on a pleasant morning in summer French departed for Georgia in his gleaming black Buick. With him as passengers were attorneys Hays and Moore. They looked forward to the trip and to the little diversions and adventures it promised.

The wreck of the other Buick a year earlier had been caused by lug nuts loosening on the bolts of a wheel while the car was at high speed. The wheel had gone spinning over the side of a hill and, after a series of jolts and jars, the car had followed it end-over-end to the bottom of a steep, brush-grown incline. It was only natural that French should now have a keen interest in the state of the nuts and bolts on all the wheels of his new Buick. Thus when he stopped for gasoline, he paid the station attendant to remove the hubcaps and tighten all the screw-on nuts. Standing above the muscular workman, French exhorted him to apply all his strength to the task. Beads of sweat and deep grunts accompanied the tightening of each wheel's five bolts. Toward the end French laid aside his coat and assisted the attendant, straining at the task with all his very considerable strength. The obsession persisted. At each and every stop southward, and back northward, the process was repeated. French was absolutely determined that he would never again experience the consequences of a runaway wheel!

In Georgia the visitors found huge, comfortable rooms in a vast, old hotel where the grits, baked ham, fried chicken, biscuits, and cornbread were superb. At ten the next morning, rested and comfortably fed, they appeared at a hearing room in the ancient courthouse. They found the place jammed with blacks, all dressed in the humble garments of men and women who lived by sharecropping the lean acres of plantation landlords. The commissioner was white, of course, with the courtesy and urbanity of a southern gentleman. In fact, every person who worked in the courthouse was white with the solitary exception of the janitor.

When the hearing had been called to order by the commissioner, the stipulations were read into the record. The depositions that followed occupied two days as a long procession of witnesses took the stand. All were black, all lived on a single plantation, all made their living planting, chopping, and picking cotton. As all were illiterate or nearly so, it was practically impossible to confine their testimony within the rules of evidence. Collectively the depositions revealed an old society in the final throes of dissolution.

The facts that emerged were these. James Wright had been born on the same plantation and had emigrated to the coal mines of Letcher County in search of a land of hope and promise. "Moma" was not his mama but was an "aunt" with whom the child's mother had left him so she could "go to town." She never returned. The "aunt" was not the mother's sister, nor was she otherwise related to the boy whom she raised. Moma was not a misspelling of Mama, as French had supposed, but was the name her mother had affixed to her at birth seventy years earlier. Yes, James Wright had sent her money from time to time; otherwise she would have starved to death.

The three common law wives were nearly the same age and were born and grew up on the same plantation described by Moma. The wife of the plantation owner was named Rosa. When each of these Rosas was born, the planter's wife had a doctor look in on the mother. Each mother gratefully named her daughter

Rosa. The three Rosas grew up more or less together on the 25,000-acre plantation. Around the age of sixteen, each suffered a similar mishap. James Wright, then about twenty, had been to Kentucky where he had learned the fundamental skills of a miner. He whispered to each Rosa in turn that he would go back to McRoberts for employment, rent a company house, and send a bus ticket and money so that she could join him. They would get married and live in the new Zion. He described the model mining town with its concrete sidewalks and paved streets, its movie house and recreation halls, and its vast commissary with huge stocks of meats, canned goods, clothing, and shoes. All these things could be bought with the brass scrip which a wife could obtain from a clerk. He described the cool green hills, the clattering tipples, and the coal trains rattling in with empties and rumbling out with mile-long strings of loaded cars. Each girl believed him and hoped desperately to escape the desolate plantation with its leached soil and lurching cabins. Each waited, of course, for the ticket and the money which never came.

But Wright went further. He took each of them to bed, not once but several times. Each woman swore it was true and produced a coal-black youngster of nine to prove it. There were even eyewitnesses who swore to at least some of their couplings. As one old man expressed it, "Can't nothin' happen in a cotton shack but everybody else can see and hear it unless he be deaf and blind." At the conclusion of the depositions the commissioner and lawyers rode out to the plantation. The bleak two- and three-room shotgun houses, tottering on wooden posts, fronted a clay-dirt road. On rickety porches the three Rosas sat, their faces blank, their eyes staring but seeing nothing. The children huddled without play. The aspect was of unrelieved lassitude and surrender.

They stopped at the house occupied by one of the Rosas and an aged couple they took to be grandparents. The old man who had sworn that he had seen his grandchild begotten had used an apt description. As J.L. Hays told me fifteen years later, "A full bulldog could have been thrown through the holes in those shacks—in one side and out the other—without turning a hair."

Harry Moore would always remember an admonition he received from the Georgia court commissioner. A New Yorker and a kindly man, Harry addressed one of the black witnesses as "Mr. Mason." This brought a sharp stroke of the gavel and "Here, here, Mr. Moore! In Georgia you don't call a nigger 'mister.' He said he is Lige Mason. From now on call him Lige!"

Their investigations and hearings finished, the three attorneys returned home, reflecting on what they had seen and heard. They pondered the irony that the depression-ridden coal fields seemed like havens of plenty compared to the somnolent country they were leaving.

Their journey was unhurried and pleasant. They stopped at points of interest along the way, and spent a night on the road in a lovely, timeless hostelry where white-jacketed black waiters served marvelous southern food, cooked in steaming kitchens by black cooks who knew the precise moment when a catfish should be lifted from a hot skillet and the exact preparation of a blackberry cobbler. All went well with them until they passed through Cumberland Gap and descended to Middlesboro, a city built by English iron masters in the 1880s, where they stopped to buy gasoline and to stretch their legs. As soon as they were on the pavement, they heard the hiss of escaping air. One of the tires had picked up a nail and the punctured innertube would have to be patched. French left the car in the hands of an immense black mechanic who promised to patch the tube and remount the wheel while the three sojourners ate supper at a nearby restaurant.

Scarcely had they found a table when the mechanic appeared at the door and made straight for their table. His chest still heaved from exertion and a stream of perspiration flowed down his forehead. Looking at French with an expression of amazement he declared with unarguable finality, "Boss, it *ain't* comin' off! That's all there is to it."

The barristers departed, their food unordered. The mechanic demonstrated the stubborn, unyielding hold of each of those six-sided screw nuts. Powerful exertion resulted in nothing but copious flows of sweat. After this failure another method was tried. Attorney Hays held the tool firmly in place while French and the mechanic put their feet against the handles of the tire tool to exert the great strength of their legs. The tool bent perceptibly, but the nut did not move. The others were equally secure.

Acknowledging temporary defeat, they spent the night in a hotel. The next morning they sought the expertise of the local Buick dealer, but not a lug nut was loosened. When tested, all the other wheels were found to be equally adamant. No wheel could be removed from that Buick.

The repeated tightening had so welded the surfaces of the nuts and bolts that they had virtually fused. Even if sufficient force could be brought to bear, the threads of the bolts would strip off, leaving them useless. One thing was sure: none of those wheels would run away to French's injury.

The rest of the journey—about eighty miles—was made by bus. The Buick dealer ordered four complete new wheel assemblies and a week or so later the Buick rested on four new wheels. An acetylene torch was used to cut off the old wheels. French rode a crowded bus back to Middlesboro to retrieve his beloved carriage. He paid the bill with much rue and continued to be cautious about wheels that come off, but never so cautious as he had been on his southern journey.

And what of the money in the estate of James Wright, a coal miner, deceased? Of course, the courts had to be paid their costs and fees. The lawyers were compensated for their efforts in behalf of their respective claimants. The administrator could justly claim a fee for his services, which included that long and wearisome trip to Georgia. Checks must be mailed to the hearing commissioner and to the court reporter. There were also, of course, charges for postage and telephone. Nevertheless a substantial residue was left for distribution.

At French's recommendation the judge entered an order finding that Wright's dependents were "Moma," who had raised him, and the three children whom he had fathered by the three Rosas. The women themselves were not dependent upon him and had no claim. The Georgia court appointed a guardian to receive the money on behalf of the three children and to "expend it for their care and nurture." The judge appointed the commissioner who had presided at the hearing "because he is already acquainted with the pertinent facts." He executed a fidelity

bond and it, along with compensation for his services, were paid
out of each child's share. Even so, for several years there was
money for new shoes, for occasional dresses and coats, for doctors
and dentist bills, and for groceries. Thus in dying, James Wright
spread both pleasure and hope, and left a legacy that reached
numerous unexpected pockets and warmed many hearts.

2. Slender Is the Thread

THE LATE JOHN YOUNG BROWN, SR., of Lexington was for nearly forty years the state's most renowned criminal lawyer. He lived and breathed lawsuits and liked nothing so much as a hard-fought criminal trial in which the odds were against him. He had a keen mind and a marvelous memory for details. A quarter century after a trial he could quote with remarkable accuracy what various witnesses swore about an issue, the objections of lawyers concerning the testimony, and how the judge ruled on its admissibility. A lawyer meeting him on the street might expect to be greeted with, "Well, how are you today? I'm glad to see you! Oh, by the way, you remind me of a trial I was in down in your county in 1942. The war was on and . . . ."

Some years before his death in 1985 John vacationed on a Caribbean cruise ship. Several Kentucky lawyers and their wives were aboard, and John almost reduced them to tears with his tales of trials and courthouse tribulations. On one occasion a newly-married, youngish lawyer was standing with his bride watching the rise of a romantic tropical moon. Before a single tender thought could be whispered, John hove alongside with, "Say, do you remember what Lord Justice Holt wrote in 1717 in a famous bottomry case? The case turned on the testimony of a twelve-year-old cabin boy who swore that he was able to see the ship sink because the moon was full." The young man's fancies were turned from thoughts of love as John Y. detailed the ruling of the lords justice, the dissenting opinions, and what might

have happened if a certain omitted question had been pro-
pounded to the cabin boy.

John and I were involved in many cases, most of them in
Letcher Circuit Court. Almost always we were co-counsel, but
on a few occasions we were on opposing sides. More often than
not John would spend the nights as my guest. He invariably
went to bed with a novel or other book dealing with the law.

In his later years I frequently urged him to write a book about
his professional career, and toward the end he talked of doing it.
He even went so far as to choose a title for the book he never
wrote: "Slender Is the Thread." This was an allusion to the
ancient Greek concept of the Goddess of Justice who holds in one
hand the swift, keen sword of retribution, and in the other the
scales by which each word and circumstance is weighed and
measured. The goddess is blindfolded so that she may not be
influenced by appearances, and the scales are suspended from
her fingers by a slender thread. His half-century at the bar had
taught John how very tenuous, frail, and uncertain is that
thread, and how easily the balance may be caused to shift from
perfect justice to imperfect result.

In one of our cases we represented a young widow whose
husband had died during surgery for a chronic stomach ulcer.
He had visited the physician only the day before, and the doctor
had said the ulcer had to be removed at once, recommending the
following day at 9:00 A.M. No electrocardiogram was made and
no case history was noted—both crucially important because the
patient's father had died of cardiac arrest during an appendec-
tomy. In this hurried fashion the patient was taken to surgery
and, like his father some twenty years earlier, died of heart
failure in the midst of the operation.

Malpractice cases were rare in the early 1960s, but we were
convinced that, under the facts of the case and the applicable
law, the widow was entitled to a substantial recovery. Actually
her demands were extremely modest by today's standards. She
sought only enough money to study to become a registered nurse
and to send her son through a moderately-priced college. The
physician was protected by an ample malpractice insurance
policy and the insurer had placed his defense in the hands of
excellent lawyers. All efforts to reach a settlement had failed

because the doctor vetoed all proposals, a right given to him under the terms of the policy.

John and I were confident of winning the case except for a single grim possibility: a jury fix. In Kentucky—especially in rural counties—there have always been shadowy figures who have arranged jury verdicts in crucial cases. Most of these people are criminals with long conviction records, some are former public officials. They know the people of the county well, have wide and detailed knowledge of the jury pool, that is the segment of the population from which the venire is likely to be chosen, and are able to identify venal jurists who can be talked to in advance. If a particular verdict is secured, money will be paid as a consideration. If the people are poor and times are hard, a job may be promised. On the other hand, the arrangement may be based on purely political considerations such as the avenging of an old political defeat. Sometimes the political consideration is purely partisan, a chance to strike a blow at a member of the opposing party or faction. In this way juries are hung when one or more jurors adamantly hold out against the evidence and in defiance of all the other jurors. Or enough jurors may be reached to swing the verdict, especially in cases where honest men and women are perplexed by contradictory testimony. All this is strictly illegal and judges routinely admonish jurors to discuss cases only with other members of the panel. In rural Kentucky, however, court cases are frequently seen as games played under the axiom "May the best man win!" Justice as an abstraction carries little weight. Consequently, good lawyers are constantly on the alert for signs of a jury fix and ways to forestall or thwart it.

It was against this background that John and I faced the trial of our malpractice case. We knew our client deserved to prevail but we sensed—almost smelled—the stench of a stacked jury.

In those days Sandusky Julian Bates was very much alive and abroad in the land. Actually his name was not Sandusky, it was Samuel. The fancy moniker was the imaginative invention of a man who was simply Sam Bates to all who knew him and his accomplishments. His remarkable career in crime came to a crashing end in 1963 when he was shot to death by a petty thug he was trying to hustle. Letcher was, and is, a dry county, and

Bates claimed to be able to secure not only the forebearance but the protection of the sheriff for a young man who had set himself up as a bootlegger. Sam had no such influence and the sheriff raided the malefactor. Sam said that this was an unfortunate misunderstanding, and extorted still another payoff. When still another raid followed, the bootlegger's indignation passed all bounds and he avenged himself by shooting his protector in the forehead with a .38-special revolver.

In his colorful career Sam was tried three times for murder and was convicted each time. One of his victims was his brother, whom he killed in a squabble over their father's will. After Sam had served time for these and other misdeeds, and after governors had pardoned him for some of his outrages and commuted his sentences for others, he combined his bootlegging with a few years in the coal business. From these enterprises he emerged rich and therefore respected. His combination of rascality, cunning, and wealth made him a power in the county. This power was ill-used, as illustrated by his frequent rigging of juries.

His motive in such endeavors is hard to explain. It is doubtful that he accepted pay for such sordid services. In some cases neither party knew that Sam was at work on the jurors who were empaneled in the case. In a civil suit Sam might simply do his work to prevent a disliked lawyer from collecting a contingent fee. In a criminal case he might seek a conviction because he held a grudge against the defendant and wanted him behind bars irrespective of guilt or innocence. Most often he tried to get a defendant acquitted, probably because he hated government with its laws and officers and courts.

In his career in crime Sam was tried for practically everything except jury tampering. Though his skill in this odious craft was well known, proof against him was never secured. Nonetheless skilled lawyers knew and tried by guiles of their own to thwart him.

A dishonest person will do good works for evil purposes. Sam was known for his generosity. If a man was jobless and penniless, a load of groceries might be received "compliments of Sam." An old lady with a sore throat and the flu oft-times was presented a bag containing a dozen lemons, a box of sugar, and a fifth of whiskey. A toddy compounded of these ingredients was recognized as a sovereign remedy. An elderly man with many children and grandchildren might be amazed to learn that Sam had stopped at the neighborhood store and paid his account in full. Many young men and women on their way to college paid their expenses with bank loans represented by notes which Sam had signed as surety. (In 1942 Sam endorsed such a note for my sophomore year at the University of Kentucky. Sam said he did it because I was "a fine young man." I remembered this when I assisted in the prosecution of his killer.) In Sam's time physicians still made house calls and Sam not infrequently paid one to take his satchel and call on an ailing citizen.

By such means as these (and his means were legion) Sam collected a great number of IOUs, and among mountain people one good turn deserved another. Sam knew how these gestures were appreciated and that his generosity was noised abroad among relatives and friends. Thus his appearance in the courtroom in earnest conversation with a plaintiff or defendant might offer an opportunity for an observant juror to repay a favor. Sam also was fully capable of talking directly to jurors about verdicts he desired. He sometimes signalled with a simple device: a sharpened wooden pencil stuck in his shirt or coat pocket. If the keen end extended upward, a verdict for the plaintiff was desired. If it pointed down, the defendant should be favored. I have seen that tell-tale pencil so displayed many times and rarely did it fail to foretell the outcome of the litigation. If interrogated by the court about such a display, Sam would have unctuously denied that it meant anything; the jurors would have sworn that they perceived no significance in such a commonplace article.

In our malpractice case we were sure of his intervention but were unable to define his purpose. His brother Jesse, then police judge of Jenkins, warned us, "Sam is against you." Both John and I had represented Sam at various times when he was before the bar. John had defended him in an income tax evasion case and I had been his lawyer on numerous other occasions. Nonetheless he was against us, and we suspected that he had reached at least four jurors of the twelve. In such a situation there would be a deadlock or the verdict would go against us.

In two days the opening statements had been made and the

witnesses had testified. At the close of the second day Judge Hays adjourned court until the following morning. In doing so he instructed the jurors to keep open minds concerning the case, to reach no conclusions about it, to talk to no one about it, to allow no one to talk to them about it—and to report to the court any attempt to do so. They were to return at 9:00 A.M. to hear the instructions of the court, the arguments of counsel, and then—and then only—to reach a decision and write a verdict.

John and I were in a quandary. We were convinced that Sam was trying to deprive our client of a just award, and that it would be done so adroitly that no trace would be left to tell the tale or justify a retrial. John chose to spend the night in a motel. His parting comment to me was, "I am going to drop in on Sam at supper time and see if I can't talk him into doing the right thing for once in his life!"

I learned later that Sam was all joviality and hospitality when he found his friend and erstwhile lawyer at his front door. He fed John sumptuously and offered him drafts of ten-year-old bourbon. He denied involvement when John declared in the forthright manner that was his trademark, "Sam, I know that you have got this jury fixed. You are on the wrong side. This little woman and her child have never done you any harm of any kind and they deserve a judgment. I want you to undo what you have done and let the jury give her a verdict."

John continued by outlining the facts that had brought the case into the court. He described the modest nature of her claim. He mentioned the sum of money that would send her through a nurse's training program, send her son through four years of college at Morehead State University, pay all the expenses she had incurred in the case, cover the costs of her husband's burial and, of course, satisfy her attorneys' fees. Sam listened in silence until John finished with, "We have been friends a long time and I want you to do this because of our friendship. I don't want to lose this case because I was blackjacked by a friend."

Predictably, the notorious rogue denied all involvement whatsoever. Yes, he was a friend of the doctor and had sort of hoped he would not have to be out any money. He knew most of the jurors and had done little favors for them from time to time. Some of them might listen to him but he had "never breathed a word to any of them." He would think about it. He wanted to do the fair thing, of course. People were wrong about him and thought he had a lot of influence which he did not in fact possess.

Sam asked for the slip of paper on which John had jotted the various sums that would add up to an acceptable remuneration. Sam said that he wanted to "study on the matter."

At nine the next morning the lawyers for the doctor gestured for John and me to meet them in a conference room. The judge agreed to a brief delay while a "certain matter" could be discussed. It developed that the attorneys had given serious thought to the issues. They and the insurance company did not want to do injury to the young widow or to her youngster. They had done some figuring. They understood from what they had learned about her that she wanted to become a nurse and eventually send her son to college. These were honorable goals. Then, too, the costs and reasonable attorney fees should be considered. They named a sum the malpractice insurer would consider just. It was precisely the same figure John had handed to Sam thirteen hours before.

Of course John and I had to confer, and then we had to explain the offer to our client. She was delighted, but we displayed some reluctance for the benefit of our adversaries. When we accepted the proposal and commended the lawyers for their fairness and integrity they were relieved and called in the doctor to tell him they thought the settlement offer should be accepted. He indignantly rejected the whole idea and declared that *any* payment was out of the question. "Under the terms of my policy you cannot make a settlement without my consent and approval," he sternly reminded them. But the lawyers had had enough. They told him, "The company would rather face a lawsuit from you than go in there and face that jury as matters now stand."

The jurors were discharged. In due time the checks arrived and the case was dismissed. John and I were paid. The widow went to nursing school and her son grew up and graduated from college. The surgeon never sued his insurer. And what of Sam Bates? "I was only a bystander," he said, "but I think the insurance company did the right thing. The doctor was just a little bit bull-headed. The jury might have worked him over pretty hard if the case had gone to them for a verdict."

Sometimes the path to justice is devious and leads to compromises that allow the lady with the scales to smile and sheathe her sword. Some adjustments may be short-lived, but even so they create new beginnings and offer opportunities for contentment to reign in situations where discord formerly held sway.

Such a situation unfolded in 1962 in the Letcher County courthouse. A black coal miner stood indicted for firing a shotgun into an occupied dwelling. There was a very lively party in progress and the house was jammed with merrymakers. The miner had cut loose with both barrels of a .12-gauge Stevens loaded with buckshot. Fortunately he aimed at the roof and no harm was done except for a gaping hole near the chimney. But the revelers left mounds of barbecued pork uneaten and much beer undrunk, and fled in terror to their respective abodes.

My client explained his plight and I sympathized with him. Even though he had been surely abused by his neighbors, he still had no defense. The reformatory at LaGrange gaped to receive him.

These were the circumstances that had brought him into the clutches of the law: His home was in a fifty-year-old coal town that had been sold to the miners. Perhaps fifty black families lived in twin rows of two-story wooden houses facing a paved street. At the upper end of the street was the "colored graded school" (an institution soon to disappear under pressure from the Great Society). At the other end was a well-kept frame building, the African Methodist Church. These were the social centers of the community in that now-vanished era. The teachers were highly esteemed as "professors," and the man of the cloth was revered as the community's counselor in all things.

The only advanced degree in the Letcher County school system in the late 1940s was held by a black janitor at a coal-camp high school. He had studied for a master's degree at the University of Cincinnati and had returned to the hills because of homesickness. The schools were segregated and no position was available in the black schools. His employment as a teacher of white children was out of the question, but the county superintendent kindly hired him to sweep and mop the floors and wash the windows in the white high school.

Twenty years ago a black community like this one was a lively place, but since then they have shriveled as parents aged and died and children matured and fled to the cities. Some of the best singing in America resounded in their churches, and the exhortations of preachers brought many to repentance—sometimes several times over as the "brothers and sisters" regained salvation after repeatedly back-sliding. Nearly all the adults were from Alabama or Mississippi and a high percentage had been educated in good schools maintained as missions by northern churches. As a rule the women were superb housekeepers and marvelous cooks. A typical summer-time party saw a pig or side of beef barbecued in a pit and served up in generous slices with beer or home brew, and heaps of fresh corn, potato salad, and cole slaw.

The watermelons were cooled in tubs of water with huge chunks of ice and were served up in mammoth pieces. Fortunate indeed was the white man who was invited to such an affair.

The man who sought my aid was famous for the frequent and generous parties he staged in his backyard. They usually began early on a Saturday afternoon with the revelry continuing to midnight. His neighbors loved his celebrations, but gradually a suspicion developed that he nurtured an undue interest in their nubile daughters. He was alleged to pick on them (not that there was evidence that they objected) and a tall, prepossessing damsel had become pregnant. She had not identified the probable father, but all suspicion was directed at my client. He was about forty-two at the time, earned high wages mining coal for Bethlehem Steel, and drove an expensive car that glittered with a high sheen. It was suspected that in that car the young ladies of the community encountered a mighty threat to their chastity.

The upshot of all this was that his neighbors began to look upon him with disfavor. He was a highly sociable creature and their attitude wounded him deeply. Mothers and fathers protected their daughters with numerous safeguards. My client felt sorely aggrieved.

Thus matters stood when, at the peak of vibrant summer, a forty-year-old widow who lived in the house next door decided to have a party of her own. She enlisted the aid of an unmarried gentleman and the barbecue pit was made ready. Personallydelivered invitations went forth to every household save one. The wife and teenage children of my client were included, but he, the father and husband who had entertained the whole community many times and at great cost, was pointedly excluded. On the designated afternoon the teachers, the preacher, the men, women, children, and stooped elders arrived in their best raiment to enjoy a festive occasion. To arrive at the party, most had to pass my client's house where he sat snubbed and lonely on the front porch. Few spoke to him. Most turned up their noses in scorn and disapproval. His injured feelings plunged him into deep sorrow. As night fell and the roasting meat reached perfection, he heard prayers of thanksgiving from the preacher, the sharpening of carving knives, and suddenly the tapping of drums. Saxophones and trumpets blared and there were laughter, banter, and the delightful voices of young women. My rejected friend grieved for his downfall. Suddenly he was overwhelmed by a mighty sense of injustice. Seizing his trusty shotgun he rushed up the hill, blasted the roof with that double charge, and thus completed his ruin. When I went to the courtroom with him I found that the entire community—all the people fifteen and older except his own wife and children—were in attendance. Outraged and indignant, they awaited the turning of the wheels of justice. Every brow was drawn down, every eye gleamed with vengefulness. The most searching look found not the slightest trace of forgiveness or friendliness.

Since 1963 the news media have displayed countless scenes of impoverished, ragged, dirty, and disheveled Appalachian white people shuffling blankly about. If asked, each of these Anglo-Saxons would have asserted his innate superiority to "niggers." Yet the blacks in that courtroom were well scrubbed, neatly dressed in stylish clothing, wore brightly polished shoes, and displayed fresh shaves and recent haircuts. They, too, were Appalachian, but the contrast between them and the region's multitudinous poor whites was startling.

It was apparent that this was no time to try my friendless, chastened client. Judges and prosecutors are elected and the outraged blacks were registered voters. With utmost difficulty I persuaded the court to grant a continuance to the next term, three months away. The commonwealth attorney inveighed mightily against my motion and, in truth, my grounds were tenuous. My client had been so depressed and shattered by the whole affair that he had failed to retain me until that morning—mere minutes before the case was scheduled for trial! But the judge was innately just and saw that, whatever had caused the defendant's dilatory attitude and behavior, a fair trial was out of the question. Over the prosecution's bitter objections the case was postponed, with admonitions that defendant and his counsel could expect no further delays. The scowls from at least one hundred black faces were sobering reminders that deep trouble lay at the end of our respite.

Back in my office I told the defendant the course he would have to pursue if those grim steel gates were not to close behind him. There was no possibility that he could win an acquittal based on the law and the evidence. His hope for deliverance lay in guile and stratagems. His face brightened as I outlined the steps he must take—steps no one else could take for him.

He must live an exemplary life for at least three months until the next term of Letcher Circuit Court had come and gone. He must not pick on any of the girls and he was to treat all his neighbors with supreme civility. He would ask the carpenter how much he had charged to repair the damaged roof and would send a check in full payment.

Then, in two weeks, he was to get himself dressed up and go to church. He must sit humbly on the back bench and listen gravely to every word the preacher said. When the service ended he was to leave promptly and discreetly. He must return in the same manner every Sunday. After a month or six weeks he was to move down a row or two so that in about ten weeks he would be at the front of the congregation. I looked at my calendar and noted a date for him: on that Sunday when sinners were called to the mourners' bench, he must rise and go. There and then he should acknowledge the sinful nature of his life and seek atonement. At another meeting he would announce his hope for baptism and regeneration. This would bring him to the Sunday before his scheduled trial.

As he listened, his eyes reflected a cunning glint. "I hate to get saved," he said, "but I can do it if that is the only way to stay out of the pen."

The weeks passed and the day of the trial was at hand. When Judge Hays ascended the bench, a look of astonishment swept across his face and he directed a long questioning look at me. I looked straight ahead with an air of righteousness.

The case was called by the clerk, and the defendant rose from his place among that same multitude that had previously come to crush him. At his side was the preacher, and they were surrounded by deacons, Sunday school teachers, leaders of the Ladies Auxilliary, and just plain seat members. The preacher asked if he might have a word with the commonwealth attorney. When the request was granted, a score of deacons, elders, and deaconesses followed the pastor into the conference room. When the prosecutor returned a quarter-hour later, he motioned for me to join him at the bench.

What prosecuting attorney Emmet G. Fields disclosed was an amazing turnaround. Whereas at the previous term the entire community had demanded trial and punishment, they now sought with complete unanimity to have the case dismissed. Most insistent of all was the lady whose roof had received the buckshot. The mother of the girl my client had allegedly seduced was now sure that he was a changed man. Her daughter, too, was forgiving. The preacher, elders, and wise men outlined the quiet, dignified manner in which their errant neighbor had sought grace and salvation. "To send a man like that to the penitentiary after God has washed his sins away would be awful wrong," the preacher opined, punching the attorney's lapel with a large, thick forefinger.

Judge Hays challenged me, "Why, last term they were mad as hell because I granted a continuance and now you say they all want the case dismissed?" My reply was that man could undergo regeneration early or late and that we should all rejoice in a sinner saved. This brought me the nastiest look I ever received from a judge. "When did this salvation hit him?" he demanded. But I replied truthfully, "I have not seen any of these people—not even my client—since we met here at the last term." Then I reminded the judge that reformation was the first aim of the law and that a man who had reformed and begun a new and moral life should not be locked up in prison. This brought a chorus of amens from the cluster of church leaders.

The judge was dubious. "Something is going on," he murmured. Nonetheless, at Mr. Fields's request he directed the clerk to compute the cost and reluctantly ordered that the case be dismissed, with all the costs to be forthwith paid by the accused.

When my client withdrew his checkbook from his pocket, the minister nudged me. We retired to one of the conference rooms followed by a long string of smiling brothers and sisters. When the door closed behind us, a shower of compliments and congratulations fell on my happy client. He was hugged by some and pounded on the back by others. The good reverend announced the sum of the court costs and a hat went round. Thus the forgiving victims paid for the sins of their persecutor. I delivered the money to the clerk and the smiling congregation departed with my client in its midst.

A couple of weeks later I encountered the good woman whose house had been attacked. I inquired about the people of her community, and most especially about the spiritual and material welfare of my former client.

Her eyes flashed fire. "Don't talk about him!" she thundered. "He has already backslid and is a-pickin' on all the young girls agin! The preacher says the devil has done got him in spite of all we could do!"

At that moment the Goddess of Justice surely sighed.

Four years later my client returned with another tale of woe. His wife was a sturdy woman of strong temper and she had become unusually enraged at him because of an escapade involving one of the young women of the neighborhood. In her wrath she had armed herself with a bargain-counter .22-calibre pistol with a barrel about one-and-one-half inches long. She had loaded it with short cartridges (bought because they were cheaper) and awaited his homecoming. When, humming softly, he entered the front door, she presented her pistol and vowed to kill him. He took flight through the kitchen and out the back door with her in hot pursuit. He fled along a path that led around a hillside to his immaculate Buick, while the wife of his bosom fired her shooting iron into his back. Neighbors reported that at each shot he emitted piercing shrieks and wails for mercy. This continued until the five cartridges in her Saturday-night special were used up and he had reached his car. He drove at break-neck speed to the Jenkins hospital where he presented himself at the emergency room with loud assertions that he had been "shot square through five times."

The surgeon commanded him to remove his blanket-lined leather jacket and his sweater and shirt, and to lie face down on the examination table. Sure enough, he had been shot five times but not "square through." The sturdy leather and woolen garments had acted as a flak jacket and the feeble cartridges fired from the anemic pistol had merely propelled the bullets part way into his shoulders. They remained "half in and half out," as the doctor phrased it, and he withdrew them with tweezers. He painted the wounds with mercurochrome, applied band-aids, and sent him forth.

My client recovered quickly. The grand jury was in session at the time and he promptly presented himself at its antechamber. Admitted to tell his tale, he described his ordeal in florid terms and showed the jurors the five bullet holes. The panel immediately returned an indictment charging his wife with attempted murder.

Before the trial could be scheduled, the pair fell in love again and the turbulent marriage was patched up. At this point he came to pay me to defend her for shooting him. In his new state of mind he yearned to keep her out of the penitentiary.

The commonwealth attorney was unsympathetic. He had read the transcript of the victim's testimony to the grand jury, and deemed her actions "a most heinous crime, a carefully-planned attempt to kill her husband." On the morning of the trial the two sat in court together, their arms entwined, her head on his shoulder. I pleaded with the prosecutor, pointing out that they had children, were reconciled, were deeply in love, that the wounds were minor, and that her conviction and imprisonment would break the hearts of her son and daughter. The victim reinforced my plea with loud and fervent affirmations.

At length the prosecutor surrendered to the realities of the case and agreed that the charge should be reduced, the defendant paying a two-hundred-dollar fine for breach of the peace. Of course she had no money, and he had to pay the fine. When this judicial proceeding had been solemnly affirmed by the judge's signature, the clerk handed my client a receipt for the fine and court costs. He stared with rueful and uncomprehending gaze at the bits of paper and sighed. "I just don't understand this law business. She shot me five times and now I have to pay over forty dollars a shot." Then, wrathfully, "It ain't fair. I don't care what anybody says."

But the demands of justice had been met. The chastised wife went back to her house and her husband went back to the coal mines.

I suspect that the lady with the scales managed a smile.

Sometimes the quest for justice is thwarted by a misplaced and overweening sense of pride. The prospect of imprisonment or even death by electrocution is deemed preferable to loss of face.

Long ago attorney Harry L. Moore and I defended a black track layer charged with murder of a fellow workman. The two were part of a labor gang that was extending the Louisville and Nashville line into a new coal field on Rock House Creek. They received their week's pay on a Saturday morning and promptly retired with a half-dozen of their brethren to a secluded place to roll dice for who should have the fruits of their collective toil. Our client was a wiry little man, about forty years old, who had deserted the cotton fields of Mississippi. By ruse or skill or simple luck his winnings grew apace amid the scowls and murmurs of the losers. One man, described as "eeenormous," doubted that a winning streak could last so long with honest dice and repeatedly said so. Our client continued to pull the winnings to his side of the table. When the "eeenormous" loser was "busted and flat-broke," he drew a pocketknife, flicked the blade out of its case and declared, "I'm agoin' to kill me a crook." Whereupon he charged around the end of the table. But before he could reach his goal the defendant pulled a snubnosed pistol from his jacket and shot him dead-center between the eyes. There was no conflict as to the facts. Every person present described the homicide just as I have related it.

Going over the evidence with our client, Mr. Moore and I emphasized that when he fired the shot he was in grave danger and that, as shown by the uncontradicted evidence, he acted in fear and as the only way to save his own life. He went through the testimony as he would deliver it from the witness chair. In this dry run of his testimony Mr. Moore looked him in the eye and demanded. "Now why did you fire the shot that killed the decedent?" Quick as a wink the reply came, "Cause I knowed he would kill me for shore. I shot him to save my own life!"

At the trial the evidence unfolded quickly. The witnesses related the events of the payday, the drawing of wages, the setting of the crap game, the defendant's unbroken winning streak, the rage of the victim and his knife-wielding attack, and the fatal shot fired at the last second. All witnesses swore on cross-examination that the defendant would most certainly have been killed by his oversized attacker if he had not fired his pistol with such superb accuracy.

Then our client took the stand. His story matched that of the other witnesses precisely. His account was straightforward and convincing. He had fired only to save his own life. Then Mr. Moore asked a final question "to cinch the proof." Looking the defendant over very carefully and pausing amid the silence of the courtroom for maximum dramatic effect, he demanded, "Tell the jurors the state of your mind at that moment when the now-deceased man was bearing down on you with that knife in his hand declaring he was going to kill you. Tell the jury whether you were in fear for your life."

Every eye in the courtroom was riveted on the diminutive black man in the huge oak witness stand, expecting a fervent avowal that he was terrified when he fired the shot that saved his life. But there was a prolonged silence. The obvious and expected answer did not come. He looked down at the floor and up at the ceiling, then studied his clasped hands. The judge said, "Answer the question!"

The witness took a long, deep breath, returning the attorney's level, stern gaze. "No, sir, I wasn't afraid of him. In fact, I ain't afraid of nothing that walks, crawls, creeps, or flies!"

The courtroom let out its collective breath. The jurors heard the judge's instructions and promptly sentenced our client to five years in the penitentiary for manslaughter—not because he was guilty, a couple of jurors later confided, but for being "a smart alec."

When we conferred with him, I asked why in the world he had returned such a preposterous answer to his lawyer's question. He said, "I shorely was afraid of him. He was a mighty dangerous man, for a fact. He woulda cut me in two if I hadn't shot him. But, now, you know how it is. I just couldn't own up that I was afraid of that nigger out there in front of all them white people! I just couldn't do it a-tall!"

In a year or two he was paroled with his pride and self-respect intact.

3. The Ultimate Judge

DURING MY TWENTY-EIGHT YEARS of law practice in Kentucky mountain courthouses I defended seventy-six murder cases and assisted in the prosecution of thirty-four others. Some of these cases involved multiple defendants so that, in all, there were 127 persons who were charged with "taking the life of another person with malice aforethought, and not in the necessary defense of his own life or the life of another person then and there present."

These killers were a varied lot who ranged in age from eleven to eighty-four years. The eleven-year old was a boy who shot his father in the top of the head. The father was bending over his wife, who writhed screaming on the floor of a coal camp house, and I have no doubt that the bullet that killed the drunken father saved the life of the terrified mother. The jury agreed and acquitted the lad after ten minutes of deliberation.

Soon after this triumph I defended another youngster—this one a little short of thirteen—who had killed his father with a blast from a .12-gauge shotgun. The father, a miner on a weekend binge and wild with the horrible fire of moonshine whiskey, had warned his wife, "I will come back and beat you to death." Midnight found the flimsy door shut against him. Growling horrid threats he found an ax and slashed the thin door into splinters. When the door crashed to the floor, the terrified woman cowered under the kitchen table. The man who had vowed to love and protect her so long as they both should live carried an open, long-bladed pocketknife in his upraised hand and his last

words were, "Oh, yes, God damn you, you are under the table. I
will cut off your head and throw it out the window!" His son
killed him with the single shell he had borrowed from a neighbor. He was acquitted as rapidly as the jury could write the
verdict.

Even sadder than these doleful tales was the episode that
brought a thirteen-year-old girl before the bar. She had killed
her stepfather in defense of her mother, a thin, stricken little
woman whose face was etched with the deepest terror and sorrow I ever saw.

All three of these children were tried in the late 1940s and
early fifties, under homicide laws much different from those of
today's code. In each case a local coal operator paid the bill for my
services.

Three other defendants were women who had killed their
husbands. All were acquitted on self-defense pleas. One of these
ladies skated on exceedingly thin ice, however. Her husband had
attempted to chastise her with slaps and cuffs, which aroused
the Cherokee blood so prominently revealed in her high-arched
nose and straight, blue-black hair. His blows unleashed a tiger.
In biblical phrasing "she put forth her hand and took up" a stout
twenty-inch piece of beech firewood. The first blow of her coun-
terattack shattered his forearm at the wrist as he sought to
shield his head. After that it was downhill for him all the way.
His ruined arm rendered him helpless and he screamed for
mercy as the blows fell on his neck, shoulders, and head. The
coroner testified that death was from "multiple, very severe
wounds inflicted with a club or other blunt implement." The
jury deliberated nearly twenty hours before returning a "not
guilty" verdict. They concluded that at the time of the killing,
"she was acting under provocation so great that a person of
ordinary prudence and restraint, acting under the same or
similar circumstances, could not have controlled her passion."
She was a tall and unusually handsome young woman, and I
have often wondered whether she remarried. If she did, I think it
likely that she was treated with more respect.

The oldest of these defendants was eighty-four. On Christmas
day in 1900 he shot a man to death in the living room of his
home. Fifty-one years later he killed another man in the same

room and with the same Winchester rifle. In both cases the jury found that he had acted in self-defense and acquitted him. In another case a seventy-nine-year-old man shot an eighty-year-old man to death in a passionate squabble over the affections of a seventy-year-old woman. In the hills sometimes the fires are banked late in life. In none of these cases was the death sentence imposed, though it might have been justified in several.

In one unforgettable case, the defendant had killed an old, defenseless black woman without provocation. He explained this dreadful act to his drinking companion of the evening by saying, "I just don't like niggers." The time and conditions precluded attempting to show that the defendant was insane. In short, he had no defense to offer and there were no ameliorating circumstances. W.A. Dougherty of Pikeville was retained as special counsel for the prosecution by black coal miners in the nearby town of McRoberts. The trial that followed was one of the most devastating psychological experiences of my life. The killer escaped the electric chair but served a long term in the penitentiary. After he was paroled, he died a slow, agonizing death of lung cancer.

I was twenty-six at the time and had just been admitted to the Kentucky bar. I had mortgaged my future to buy the law library of recently-retired Lewis E. Harvie, and had opened my office in November 1948. The case was scheduled for the January 1949 term of Letcher Circuit Court. I had never tried a lawsuit of any kind. To my dismay, Judge Sam Ward called me to his office and told me he was appointing me to defend that most pernicious of killers. In addition to his depravity, the man was a pauper who could pay nothing. In those days there were no public defenders in Kentucky and no appropriations to defray costs incurred by court-appointed lawyers. The appointee worked for nothing and paid out of his own pocket for transcripts, travel, telephone, physicians' charges, and all other outlays essential to an "adequate" defense.

I was staggered by every aspect of the task—the heinous nature of the alleged crime, the general and deep hostility to the defendant prevalent throughout the county, my total inexperience, and the substantial financial burden which, in my destitute state, I was wholly unprepared to assume.

Judge Ward, whose forty-five years in courthouses had carried him through countless lawsuits, laughed in honest glee at my shocked and crestfallen reaction. "Now, don't let it worry you," he advised. "Just do the best you can. Nobody in the county thinks he can be acquitted and most people think he will get the chair. So they won't blame you in any way for a conviction. But you are green—green as a gourd. When you go through this trial and fight Daugherty and the commonwealth attorney, you will come out with what you need most—experience. You'll get experience and I don't mean maybe! Go fight for the man just as hard as you would if you were being paid a big fee. Save his no-account carcass from the electric chair if you can, and you will be talked about as a good lawyer." He lit up one of the thousands of cigarettes he chain-smoked and his eyes twinkled. "I'll tell you something else," he confided. "If they get too hard on you, I'll help you out a little. The court can do that, you know, if it can keep from being too obvious about it!"

I had two weeks in which to get ready for this showdown with two of the ablest lawyers in the state. Commonwealth Attorney Gus Cornett was a keen legal strategist and an able speaker. He was logical and well-organized in his interrogations and arguments. In later years he would cap his career with being a competent state senator. As to the co-prosecutor, "Wad" Daugherty, he was nothing short of formidable. He was about seventy-two at the time and had practiced law for half a century. In his long career he defended more than a thousand people on murder charges—the all-time record for Anglo-American jurisprudence. In addition, he prosecuted scores of others. Daugherty spoke and acted like Abraham Lincoln, albeit smooth-shaven and bald-headed. He lived for the law and classical literature—reams of which he could recite from memory. His practice had been in the federal courts and in the state courts of Kentucky, Virginia, and West Virginia. He could cite hundreds of cases from memory and carried a working legal library in his head. Later, when I tried cases with him as co-counsel, he would sometimes write a case citation on a slip of paper and ask me to go for the book. Invariably his memory was correct as to dates, names of parties, rulings of the prevailing majority, and the views offered in dissent. Daugherty was a legendary figure and

I, poor, ignorant, inexperienced and frightened, was about to tackle him in my first court trial. At the mere thought my throat went dry and my heart raced.

The only thing I had going for me was that I had no other cases and was able to spend full time getting ready for this one. I thoroughly investigated the facts and what I learned was so appalling that I dared not permit the defendant to testify in his own defense. Cornett and Daugherty would simply dismember him. They would pick at him until his own testimony placed him in that big, oak chair Warden Jess Buchanan kept in fine shape in the state pen at Eddyville. A friend of the defendant who had seen the murder had already turned state's evidence in the hope of saving his own life. My only chance of having my first client escape the chair was to keep him silent and persuade the jury that they should show mercy. I shivered at the prospect of W.A. Daugherty—who would make the last argument—towering over the jurors as he carefully demolished both me and my neophyte defense.

Out of my harried efforts a strategy emerged. It was a poor one, no doubt, and promised the most awful consequence if it failed. At the close of the commonwealth's evidence I would offer none, then plead with the jury for a life sentence. To this end I prepared what I thought was a convincing presentation with apt quotations from the Book of Books, the King James Bible. In Douglas's *Forty Thousand Quotations* I found the support of sages, saints and statesmen. I knew that Daugherty would belittle my urgings, that he would paint a graphic picture of the murder, the dying gasps, the cruelty of an innocent life snuffed out, ending with a dramatic plea for punishment proportionate to the crime—"a life for a life." Daugherty had memorized hundreds of quotes that would justify a death sentence and so had no need to look them up for the occasion.

The trial went off quickly. The jurors were chosen in about four hours. One or two had been dismissed by Cornett because they admitted that they would not vote for a death sentence. All averred that they were without prejudice and would base their verdict on the evidence and the court's instructions. The defendant would, they said, stand innocent in their minds until and unless the presumption of innocence was overcome by the evidence. All said they could impose the death sentence but would do so only if the proof of guilt was clear and without adequate mitigation. I studied their faces for indications of solidifying opinion but they were inscrutable. The panel consisted of a school teacher, a couple of country merchants, several farmers, and some coal miners. One thing was certain: this was a "hanging jury" and it would be difficult to soften their instinctive inclinations. The testimony of the witnesses was concluded by five o'clock and the jury retired under guard until nine the next morning. The night was sleepless and filled with dread—the kind of night trial lawyers experience to the end of their careers.

The courtroom was packed to its windows and doors the next morning when Judge Ward gavelled the session to order. The jurors were in their old-fashioned swivel chairs, their faces as forbidding as before. Judge Ward was courteous and deliberate as he asked counsel whether we were ready to proceed. As three voices replied, "We are, your Honor," hundreds of eyes were fastened on us. As was customary in those years, people had come from all parts of the county to observe the drama of the judge's charge, the arguments of the lawyers, and, finally, the return of the jurors to the courtroom, the handing up of the verdict, and the hushed voice of the clerk as he read it. The solemnity was vastly accentuated by the likelihood that in this case the verdict would include fixing "his punishment at death in the electric chair." A profound silence fell when Judge Ward rapped again and announced, "Counsel for the defendant will make the opening argument!"

When I stood up, my head swam with tension. Stepping to the central place before the jury I felt myself the most insignificant person in the world; I yearned to be alone on some distant hilltop. All the fine allusions and quotations I had assembled were gone from my memory. At that horrible instant my mind became empty, totally without plan, strategy, or purpose.

As I stared blankly at the set jaws of my opponents, the implacable faces of the jurors, and the blur that was the audience, I steadied. Unbidden and unexpected, a line of poetry from Henry Wadsworth Longfellow came to my mind: "Our hearts like muffled drums are beating funeral marches to the grave." I have no idea where it came from or why. I had learned the poem in the seventh grade and now a crucial passage gripped me. All that I beheld was transient, doomed, pathetic. Within a few years judge, clerk, lawyers, jurors, defendant, and on-lookers would be dead. Nothing would remain, not even a memory. I had found the overwhelming certainty of our lives, and now I seized it as a tool to extend for a few years the life of a murderer. In scarcely more than the second required for a camera to flash, the whole scope of my presentation was completed in my mind. Such was never to happen again, but this time a surge of confidence assured me that it would work. I could have talked for hours, but I compressed my argument into about ten minutes.

In a low voice, and without any of the arm-waving histrionics so often encountered in courtrooms, I made my plea. As nearly as I can remember, it was about as follows:

> Gentlemen of the jury: You have listened attentively to all the evidence in this case and to the judge's instructions on the law. Consequently, I will not discuss either because I am sure you will remember both the evidence and the law, and will apply them fairly and justly in your deliberations. Gentlemen, the issue you now must try is not guilt or innocence. Guilt has been proved and cannot be denied. The real issue lies in the punishment you are to impose, that is whether the defendant is to die by *your* hands or live to another day when God Almighty shall say "Enough!"
>
> You may sentence him to death in the electric chair. It is within your power to do so. I plead with you now to let that dreadful punishment pass over him. Actually, he is already under a sentence of death that was imposed upon him by his creator when Adam and Eve defied their maker. Each of you, and the judge on the bench, the witnesses, every spectator out in this crowd—and every person everywhere in the world— must surely die! And after that, the judgment!

A great American poet said it well: "Our hearts,
like muffled drums, are beating funeral marches to
the grave!"

Here I paused and put my right hand over my heart, the fore
and second fingers tapping alternately at the rate of my pulse—
tap-tap-tap, a gesture I continued throughout the rest of my
remarks. The jurors had begun to pay strict attention and to stir
uneasily.

At the beginning each of us had so many days and
nights allotted him on this earth—and we have seen
many of them pass away. We are like the parking
meters on the street. A nickel is put in the slot and it
measures off an hour and then the meter hand is still.
In our case God inserted the lovely coin of life into our
hearts and the hours and the days of our years tick off
until, in God's good time, no more are left to us.
   Our hearts are truly like drums muffled for funerals—our own funerals. We do not hear them, so silently do they beat, but they are wearing out. At any
moment one may stop—here and now, or tonight or
tomorrow. When we leave this place and scatter to our
homes news will soon come that some here today have
died—and the reports of deaths will continue until all
of us are dead.
   I may die tonight on my way home. One of you may
die on this day or the next. The judge above me on the
bench may depart from us. [Here Judge Ward cleared
his throat uneasily.] The prosecuting lawyers will
both die—in a few years at most. Think of it, gentlemen. God has given this defendant life, and he
wrongfully used it to take the life of an innocent
person. But that he defied Holy Writ should cause us
to obey it the more strictly. For we know that when
Moses came down from the mountain he carried a
marble tablet on which God had written, with the

finger that gave us all life, the words, *"Thou Shalt Not Kill!"*

God has already written a sentence of death against the name of this poor foolish, misguided man. He will surely die! Do not, I beg you, write a new sentence of the same kind. Instead, lock him up at the Eddyville penitentiary so long as that muffled drum in his bosom shall beat. When it stops, this case will have ended forever. Then he shall answer to One more implacable than any executioner the state can employ.

I stopped and looked about. It was apparent that everyone had become painfully aware of his own beating heart, and of his mortality. The jurors looked at their shoes, at the ceiling, at the floor. Here and there a finger felt a chest. I closed with a final plea.

Mr. Daugherty is the best and most experienced criminal lawyer in Kentucky, and this is my first case. He will argue eloquently for a verdict of death, but I think you know in your hearts that the verdict should be for life!

I knew that those men were Bible readers and true believers in the old-time religion of the Primitive and Regular Baptists. To them every word within the Bible was true. And they could be as stubborn as an oak rooted on a Kentucky ridge. I felt pretty good when I sat down.

Mr. Daugherty was taken aback. He had not expected such a plea and had to improvise. He was occasionally eloquent and vehement, but for "Wad" Daugherty his argument was subdued and not a stellar performance.

The jury left the room and returned in a little more than an hour. I was drained of emotion and could only sit in wonderment when the clerk announced, "We, the jury, do agree and find the defendant guilty of willful murder, and fix his punishment at life in the penitentiary."

The defendant looked at me and said nothing. Never, then or later, did this wicked man say thank you, but I did receive a compensation that was priceless. Mr. Daugherty called me that night from his hotel room and congratulated me on my victory. "You did a good job in mighty hard circumstances," he said. "You have every right to be pleased."

But what did the blind-folded Lady with the scales think of it?

4. The Courts of the Squires

IN THE 1970s the Kentucky judicial system underwent extensive reform. A new appellate tribunal, the Supreme Court of Kentucky, was established and several petty courts, including quarterly courts, municipal police courts, and the courts of justices of the peace, were abolished. Such local courts generally were conducted by non-lawyers who, as often as not, ignored the Kentucky statutes and devised their own laws. Under the reform law the functions of these courts were assumed by new district courts whose judges had to be licensed attorneys. This change assured some degree of uniformity and attention to precedent but swept away much of the color and minor drama that marked county courthouses, city halls, and other assorted meeting places where the squires had dispensed justice.

The old judicial system was patterned after England's before the landing at Jamestown in 1607, when English wealth consisted largely of land. Only the eldest son could inherit land, so estates remained intact for centuries. As yeoman farmers sold their small holdings for cash and moved to the cities, estates expanded. Because only landowners could vote, which eliminated all women, craftsmen, tradesmen, and laborers, all officials came from the class of established, conservative, landowning elder sons. They were referred to as esquires, which literally means that they qualified as attendants or shield-bearers of knights. In each shire, an esquire was elected by his fellows to serve as justice of the peace. The king appointed an agent or "shire-reeve" to execute royal orders and keep an eye on the esquires. Eventually English shires became Norman counties, the esquires became just plain squires, and the shire-reeves emerged as sheriffs.

The institution of the squire's court, attended by the sheriff or his deputy, was brought to America. The Revolution democratized the institutions, which survived as peoples' courts. Here the common folk could turn for warrants against petty offenders and sue for minor damages. Anyone who could vote became eligible to act as judge, and automatically acquired the title squire, though the office rarely went to anyone under forty-five or fifty who had not demonstrated skill at lining up votes in the precincts of his district. A fiscal court could establish from four to eight judges per county. The squires of rural Kentucky mirrored the mores and achievements of their constituents, which meant that they tended to be poorly-educated, narrow-minded, conservative, and keenly partisan. Nonetheless, most of the squires I knew would almost always come down on what they deemed to be the side of justice, a process that sometimes required much dickering and wrangling as the judge strove behind the scenes to placate both sides in advance of his rulings.

I began practicing law in eastern Kentucky a quarter-century before the last Kentucky squire discarded his long-superseded edition of Baldwin's Revised Kentucky Statutes and retired to other pursuits. Here and there an old man is still greeted as squire by someone who remembers that he was once a judge.

(It should be noted parenthetically that Daniel Boone's father was a justice of the peace in North Carolina. He liked the title so well that he named Daniel's brother "Squire." Squire Boone was a baptist preacher and, like Daniel, was a renowned Indian fighter.)

In the late 1940s and the 1950s, before government spending caused flurries of inflation, young lawyers were willing to accept fees of twenty to fifty dollars for appearances in J.P. courts. Such sums would be sniffed at by today's barristers, but in those days a few such fees equaled a month's salary for a school teacher or state policeman, so I and other neophytes frequently spent Saturday mornings before the squires. Two such justices sat in

the Letcher County courthouse, their districts having been so
fashioned that the line separating them ran along the main
corridor of the building.

Squire Jess Day had served long before in the legislature and
had used the ties of a prodigious kinship to gain election and
repeated re-election as a justice of the peace. The office gave him
a prestigious seat on the fiscal court that spent the county's
money. His one-room office was piled high with an accumulation
of ancient, dust-covered papers. The floor was stained with
tobacco juice and the windows were dimmed by films of coal soot.
On his desk lay a 1940 edition of the state's statutes.

Judge Day occupied a dirty swivel chair which, when new,
had been the pride of his cousin, County Judge Henry "Hen"
Day. Now it was scuffed and scarred, and from its place behind a
venerable oak desk piled to its outermost limits with worthless
papers, the squire heard complaints, administered oaths, and
handed down decisions. He and his office typified the institution. Though we lawyers worked hard to abolish the court, it is
difficult to remember it without a fleeting pang of nostalgia.

The court and the peace officers who attended it were known,
in the terminology of their time, as fee grabbers. The squire
received five dollars for issuing a warrant or a summons in a
civil case, and the constable or deputy sheriff who arrested the
defendant or served a civil summons was entitled to a similar
fee. In civil cases these "court costs" were paid by the losing
party, but in a misdemeanor criminal case the costs could be
taxed only against the defendant, and then only if he entered a
plea of guilty or was convicted by a six-man jury. Each juror was
paid fifty cents for hearing a case. Understandably the squires
and their constables and deputy sheriffs favored convictions. It
was not uncommon for a jury leaning toward acquittal to inquire
whether they would get any pay if they turned the defendant
loose. Sometimes a negative reply would result in a prompt
conviction.

In those days adultery was frowned on, to be sure, but the
vigor with which violators were pursued perhaps had more to do
with the willingness of the accused parties to pay fines quietly.
With a promise from the court to keep all the documents confi-

dential, notoriety was avoided. Thus it was that constables, deputy constables and deputy sheriffs roamed the land in search of "violators," especially those who violated the seventh commandment. They became exceedingly skilled at detecting suspicious signs, and many poor sinners finding themselves hailed before a squire were humiliated and faced a troubled marital future. In such circumstances the quest for justice took some strange turns indeed.

One Saturday morning a constable backed his car off the highway and concealed it in bushes in a lonely spot on the south slope of the Pine Mountain opposite a still-usable logging road that entered the trees and wound along the mountain "bench." Within minutes a new, brightly-polished, dark red 1950 Dodge hove in sight. The driver was a well-dressed man of about forty-five. The woman beside him was neat and attractive and a year or two younger. It was the kind of bright day in May of which Tennyson wrote, "a young man's fancy lightly turns to thoughts of love." What followed indicates that a middle-aged man and woman can be similarly influenced by the vernal season.

The deputy waited about ten minutes, then drove after them. The tree branches crowded upon the trail, offering concealment for any forbidden deed. Within a few moments he stopped his car and proceeded silently on foot. Presently he spotted the Dodge before him. As he explained to Squire Day when he presented the crestfallen pair and swore to a warrant, "I caught them in the act, dead center."

They asserted their innocence and the trial was scheduled for the next Saturday at 10:00 A.M. The pair presented themselves at my office and asked me to defend them. The man did the talking and a stumbling account it was. I agreed to assist them but was at a loss for a tenable defense. "What can we tell the jury?" I asked. "You admit that you were caught by the constable while having sexual intercourse!"

The man looked intently at the toe of his polished shoe. After a moment of reflective silence, the woman cleared her throat. "Mr. Caudill," she said, "this is the most embarrassing thing I ever heard of and we both ought to be horse-whipped. The truth is that we have been married for twenty-two years! We have two

children in high school and a daughter in college!" Handing me
their marriage certificate she inquired, "What in the world are
we going to do?"

I left them in my office and called on the squire. He was as
astounded as I had been. Obviously adultery had not occurred,
nor had any indecent act in a public place, since their indiscre-
tion had transpired on a remote, untraveled trail in the midst of
a forest. The marriage certificate had been duly recorded and
bore the Harlan County clerk's seal and certificate of authen-
ticity. After three or four thoughtful minutes a wistful smile
flitted across the judge's face. He wrote an order of dismissal
across the warrant and handed me the money they had left with
him as an appearance bond. As I rose to leave, he asked me to
give my clients some advice: "Tell them to wait from now on
until they get home!"

"Some things are hard to believe," he said wistfully, despite
the experiences of his seventy-five years. "But then, when a man
is forty-five and has a pretty wife. . . ," and the case was closed.

Another adultery case before the same squire took an even
more bizarre turn. The man, about forty, had a good job and was
college educated and quite happily married. This did not prevent his leaving the path of righteousness to "play around" with
a young woman whose husband had gone to Detroit to "make
cars." They were taken *in delectu* by a zealous deputy. Squire
Day affably offered to impose the minimum fine and court costs
in return for a plea of guilty. The woman shrugged and offered
no demurrer, but the man was adamant. Under no circumstance
would he admit guilt.

Back in my office he explained his plight. His wife had heard
about his escapade and "the fat was in the fire." "If I am found
guilty," he said with the utmost certainty, "my wife will divorce
me. She will get custody of my children and will take my home,
and I will be out on the road like an old bum." Then, pressing
hundred dollar bills into my hands, he concluded, "I have just
got to win this case no matter what it takes!"

He and his co-defendant vowed to "outswear" the deputy—
two witnesses for innocence to one for guilt, the kind of ratio that
always holds hope of victory in a Kentucky courtroom. My
consternation was boundless when I learned a couple of days

later that his friend had deserted him. She had slunk into the squire's office, changed her plea, paid a fine and costs, and slipped away with a promise from the court that she would not be summoned to testify at the trial of her co-defendant. By this action she doubtless hoped to preserve her own imperiled marriage.

To say that my client was shaken by this development would be a mighty understatement. Shaken, yes, but still unbowed. On the day appointed he vigorously testified that he was innocent, that he had been framed by a greedy officer, that he loved his wife far too much even to contemplate such an act, and generally strove to rebut the evidence against him with volume, vehemence, and passion. And well he might, for in a prominent place sat his stern-faced wife taking in each word with an expression that boded ill.

The county attorney and I made the tired old rafters of the courthouse reverberate with our oratory. We both quoted the Bible, Shakespeare, John Bunyan, and other assorted authorities on guilt and innocence where philandering husbands were concerned. Neither of our speeches, nor the testimony of the witnesses, nor the fact that the woman had already admitted guilt moved the jurors in the slightest. They could see that the survival of the defendant's home, his domestic tranquility, his years with his children as they grew up would be stripped from him by a guilty verdict. After about five minutes of deliberation they returned with, "We the jury do agree and find the defendant not guilty."

Thus we had a very curious situation. A man and woman had been charged in a Kentucky court with the crime of adultery. The official record showed that she was guilty and he was not. In other words, it had been adjudged that at a certain time and place a woman had had illegal sexual intercourse with a man, but he had not had sexual intercourse with her! A Kentucky court had quite legally come to an impasse, a veritable dilemma from which neither party would appeal.

A few days later, asking me to come by his office, the squire asked me whether I knew the woman's whereabouts. When I said that I could find her, he handed me a check for a sum equal to the fine and costs she had paid. "See that she gets this," he admonished. "You see, a mistake has been made. She said that she did, but the jury said that he did not. Now she could not unless he did, too. Either she or the jury is mistaken. The jury verdict stands and there can be no appeal. Therefore, it is clear that she was mistaken. She forgot what happened and got mixed up in her mind and entered a guilty plea. She is entitled to have her money back, and the fine is hereby remitted."

When I handed the money to her a few days later she was delighted. "I am going to buy a bus ticket to Detroit with this," she smiled.

Once I saw the patience of Squire Day sorely tried. There was a character in town known as "Red" Prichard, an able carpenter, paperhanger, and painter whose skills were much in demand at high wages. The trouble with Red was that he was prone to drink too much, get himself arrested for public intoxication, jailed for a day or two, then fined. This occurred so many times that the squire and his cousin, Deputy Sheriff Clark Day, resolved to punish him so severely that he would "learn his lesson for good." The deputy watched Prichard closely and one morning beheld him impudently walking through the hall of the courthouse with a sagging hip pocket that indicated a whiskey bottle. He went to the squire and obtained a search warrant. When Prichard was accosted, he strongly protested but was searched anyway. In the pocket of his paint-besmirched overalls was a pint whiskey bottle of the kind used by moonshiners—and it was nearly full of a colorless liquid. Obviously Old Red was guilty of possessing moonshine whiskey, a crime for which he could be heavily fined and jailed for thirty days. The squire studied the offensive bottle standing boldly on his desk and said, "I will have to be hard on you this time, Red."

But Red demanded a trial, a jury trial. Both squire and deputy were startled. "Surely you don't think a jury would turn you loose! The liquor is right there," the squire grumped. "A jury will treat you worse than I will when they learn the facts."

But Red was adamant. A trial was scheduled forthwith. Jurors were summoned. Red defended himself and the county attorney represented the state. Eleven jurors were questioned and excluded for one reason or another. Four hours were consumed in seating and swearing a six-man panel. Late in the afternoon Clark Day was called and sworn to tell the truth, the whole truth, and nothing but the truth. He then recounted the discovery of the sagging pocket, the issuance of the search warrant, the search and discovery, the arrest, and the arraignment. He identified the bottle and the fiery white-lightning contents so ardently denounced by both Kentucky and United States statutes.

When Red took the stand in his defense, he picked up the bottle and shook it. Then he turned to the jury and said, "No bead!" He opened the bottle and sniffed it, "No smell!" He tilted it back and took a sip, "No taste!" He passed it to the jurors. "It's a bottle of water, gentlemen, and this fee-grabber deputy wants me to pay a fine and go to jail for it."

Neither the squire nor the deputy had bothered to open the bottle but had made the logical assumption that what looked like whiskey and was contained in a bottle made for whiskey *was* whiskey. Red was discharged by the squire with the admonition, "You are a smart alec!" The deputy promised, "I will lay for you!" As for Red, he went home full of triumph and elation, and for several days his feat was the talk of the town.

In my experience jurors generally have the good sense to disregard the vapidities and repetitions that pass for "arguments of counsel" and, not infrequently, treat the convoluted instructions of judges in the same way. I doubt that I ever heard a more laudable judicial instruction than that invariably given by Squire Day. Opposing lawyers usually submitted written instructions which they thought embodied the law. After reading them with painstaking care Day would lay them aside and say to the panel of "good men and true" (women did not serve as jurors in the Kentucky hills in those days), "Gentlemen of the jury, you have heard all the witnesses testify and have listened to what the lawyers had to say. Now go into the jury room and, to the best of your ability, write a verdict that will do justice to both sides and all the parties."

Rules of evidence could be fashioned by a squire in the same cavalier manner. In the court of "Prayin' " Bob Sexton I once complained bitterly that my client was being tried without factual evidence and solely on rumors and hearsay. He glared at me, pounded his desk with a stout stick that served as a gavel, and brusquely declared, "You are overruled! I have been hearing these rumors, too!"

I tried a memorable case in his court early in the Korean War. A comely young woman lived with her two-year-old daughter in a tumble-down house at the head of a hollow while her husband fought the Koreans. A young man was seen going to her shack with a stovepipe late on a blustery November day. Watchful neighbors, concerned that one of our country's defenders might be cuckolded, reported that, after the new pipe had been installed, smoke came out of the flue. Then, they noticed the lights were turned off and the place was immersed in darkness and silence.

When a couple of indignant officers armed with one of Prayin' Bob's warrants pounded on the door, they heard a "pilin' around noise" inside and found both man and woman standing by the hot stove dressed only in underwear. They were promptly cast into the Neon town jail (often reputed to be "the worst jail this side of hell") where they and the child were incarcerated securely until the next day.

The man's father paid my fee and asked me to represent both defendants. In an earlier time he had served many years as constable in the district and knew the ropes. I dreaded to face the indignation of jurors and a J.P. whose own relatives were fighting alongside the wronged husband, but the one-time guardian of the law assured me that all was well. "I can practically g'yarntee they will come clear," he opined.

At the trial pleas of not guilty were entered and, upon my motion, a disinterested deputy who had not been involved in the raid (and who conveniently just happened to be present) was directed to summon a panel of jurors. A considerable crowd was in attendance, but the officer went far and wide in a scrupulous search for veniremen who were without knowledge of the case and had no opinion one way or the other. More than four hours passed in this search for jurors, a delay that sorely vexed Prayin' Bob. After the county attorney had exhausted his challenges, my clients faced trial before the most disreputable group of jurors I have ever beheld. Without exception they were dirty in both person and clothing. Three had served time for making moonshine whiskey. Another had killed his brother in a squabble over a potato patch. Of these four, one sat beside his son and another by his son-in-law. It was apparent that the lady with the scales faced a severe test that day.

The officers described their raid. They had arrived at nine o'clock. A chilly rain was falling and the house was in darkness. When the door was opened at their demand, the stove was blazing merrily and the chagrined defendants were meagerly dressed—she in a slip and he in nothing more than his undershorts.

The defendants swore that they were innocent of adultery. The stovepipe had rusted and had to be replaced. The man had volunteered to do the job, "mainly for my old buddy in Korea." When the new pipe was in place and the house warmed by a fresh fire, he gathered his tools to depart. Suddenly, to his dismay the downpour began. Weary from his labors he accepted her invitation to spend the night on the sofa. A blanket was spread on the couch in the cozy heat of the stove. He laid aside his damp clothes, snuggled under the blanket and fell into a weary slumber. She went to bed with her infant in another room. So they slept in complete innocence until the stern voice of the law rang out and heavy fists beat on the door.

The onlookers seemed as dubious of this tale as I was, which was very dubious indeed, but the jury needed only three or four minutes to hand in a verdict of acquittal.

After justice had so triumphed, the ex-constable and I discussed the matter in my car. He explained our victory in this way: "Well, you see, you can win any case, no matter how hard the facts, if you have the right jury. In every community there are people who would acquit Judas Iscariot if you know where to find them. I arranged to have that pertickler deputy here to summon them, and I gave him a list of names. He had a hell of a time finding some of them because they had gone off over into Pike County but he got 'em, and they qualified, and that's all there is to it!"

"But how did you persuade him to do you such a favor?" I demanded. "He spent nearly all day on the case and, since they were found not guilty, there will be no taxation of costs and he will get no pay."

He shifted his cud of tobacco from one side of his mouth to the other before replying. "Say what you will about that woman, she is mighty good lookin' and not a day over twenty-six. She told me to tell him that if he would bring in a jury that would turn them loose she would go to bed with *him*."

The scales fell from my eyes and I perceived.

Of all my clients who suffered the wrath of the law because of extramarital temptations, none paid a heavier penalty than a youngish skilled workman (whom I shall properly call a craftsman) who sought my help in a divorce case. He hobbled into my office on crutches, his left leg encased in a plaster cast far above the knee, his face and hands lined and inflamed with long and deep lacerations. He was scarcely able to move and his joints popped with a stiffness one would expect of a man who had passed four score. He sank into a chair and heaved a deep sigh as he handed me a copy of the divorce complaint and summons. There were allegations of adultery, infidelity, and cruelty, and a demand that the court award his wife their house and its furnishings, an automobile, custody of the children and, for their support, nearly all his anticipated income. "I'm destroyed, just plain destroyed," he allowed in a lugubrious voice.

The tale, as he unfolded it, was doeful indeed. It seems that among his neighbors were a large, strong-minded truck driver and his attractive wife. My client decided that while the former was hauling coal, he could seduce the latter, and could accomplish it all so dexterously that neither wronged spouse would ever be the wiser. His own wife worked as a nurse on the night shift at a nearby hospital. A coal boom was underway and the trucker's Big Mack ran from three in the afternoon to midnight. My client's deft overtures were rewarded and in due time an assignation was arranged. At eight o'clock on the evening appointed he would pick up his willing neighbor and take her in his spotless new Buick to a lonely, unfrequented road.

So adroitly was all this managed that the craftsman could pride himself on his finesse. Unfortunately for him, the truck driver was both deeply suspicious of his wife and keenly observant of things in general.

The summer evening of their clandestine meeting was heavy

with thunderclouds. She slipped into his car at the designated time and the Buick whisked them to the abandoned road. The trail left the highway in a hill gap and the trees formed a leafy tunnel through which they crept with lights dimmed. When he stopped the car, they were in total darkness, broken only by occasional light from the approaching storm.

To borrow a phrase from Burton's *Tales from the Arabian Nights,* he began to "toy and dally" with his acquiescent neighbor, but he did not toy and dally very long. Suddenly mingled with the rumble of thunder could be heard the roar of a Mack truck. Making his way with only the lightning to guide him, the wronged husband bore down upon them. When the truck halted behind them, my client departed in great haste. He escaped at the precise moment when the lightning exhausted itself and a mighty wind and a deluge of rain fell upon the little drama. Within seconds he was so soaked that even his shoes overflowed. In the tomblike darkness he plowed down the hill and the truck driver shot in the direction of the noises he made. As the bullets from the .45 automatic buzzed by him, our hero broke clear of the woods into an ancient regrown field where he was scratched and torn from all directions by huge blackberry briars and low-growing saw briars. From a hundred gaping tears his blood flowed out to mingle with the rain and the perspiration arising from terror and exertion.

He was dressed in a short-sleeved shirt and thin summer trousers, which were no protection from the bite of the briars and brambles. A long saw-toothed vine cut deeply into his nose and forehead. He felt warm blood pouring down his legs, arms, and face. He was nearly felled by a thick grapevine which struck his chest like a taut steel cable. Then, more horrible still, his left leg was suddenly seized above the ankle in a vise-like grip. No struggle however great could shake off the monster holding him, and he dared not reach down to determine its nature. In fact he was afraid to move at all, in any direction. Below was the nameless, faceless menace and above, sailing by his head and shoulders, the bullets whined until the last cartridge was expended. The trucker directed a few choice oaths at him, drubbed his now-penitent spouse, and dragged her into the cab of the Big Mack. He revved the engine until it roared and rammed the Big

Mack into the back of the prim Buick, crumpling the trunk compartment like so much tinfoil. At this point the trapped man collapsed and fell to the ground, excruciating pain piercing his leg as it fractured between knee and ankle. With the strength of the desperate he groped in the darkness to find the diabolical trap into which he had blundered. To his astonishment he felt the round outline of an ancient galvanized tub of a kind once used at all moonshine stills. Abandoned upside down, it had rusted over many years. When my fleeing client trod upon it, his foot broke through and the tired metal found new life and held him with the tenacity of a bear trap.

With bleeding hands he managed to draw back the crumpled edges. Moaning with agony as he balanced on his sound leg, he extracted his dangling foot. Lowering himself to the leafy ground he crawled about in search of a stick, praying fervently all the while that he would not put his hand on a rattlesnake instead. To his indescribable relief he found a fallen tree branch about six-feet long, sturdy and undecayed. Using it as a crutch, his mangled leg hanging limply like a dead man on a gallow, he groped his way down the rough slope, through bushes, around trees, and past large rocks. The rain abated to a steady drone and cold sweat continued to join the water and blood. He sat frequently on the soaked earth to rest, rising each time in torment and anguish to press on toward the state road. After what seemed an eternity he saw headlights passing, and four hours after he had avoided the last bullet he dragged himself to the edge of the pavement.

By that time it was nearly two o'clock on a Saturday morning and passing vehicles were few. The first driver slowed for a hurried look and sped on. The apparition which showed itself in his headlights was dressed in tatters. Long slits in its trousers revealed bloody legs. Little was left of its shirt. It balanced on one foot and leaned on a long, stout cudgel. Its head and face were red with blood and its eyes were round and bright like a Jack O'Lantern's. The driver drove to the nearby town of Jenkins and told the first policeman he encountered that a ghost or a dead man was standing by the roadside a couple of miles back.

Police rescue people from the consequences of every conceivable folly, and soon the protecting arm of the law was extended to this devastated sufferer, who was delivered to the emergency room of the local hospital. The officer was much puzzled by the claim of a man he had known for years, and deemed to be respectable, intelligent, and hard-working, that he could remember nothing whatever of the awful catastrophe that had befallen him.

While the doctor and his assistant bathed, bandaged, sewed up, and set in plaster the various wounds before them, the poor shattered fragment of humanity struggled to explain his singular adventure. As he strove valiantly to retain some measure of coherence under the bright lights and inquiring eyes who should enter the room but his own wife, after hours of dutiful labor in the wards. She stared in disbelief at the condition of the man she had kissed good-bye a few hours earlier. His eyes met hers; his frayed nerves snapped; he moaned and fainted into the warm sheltering folds of unconsciousness.

As he slowly healed in body and spirit, he sought by every conceivable means to placate her. He had never considered the possibility that she would learn of his philandering. He had told himself that he would have his cake and eat it too. Now harsh reality was about to deny him both women, impoverish him, and make him the laughing stock of half a county. His was the most doleful expression I ever saw.

I could not properly discuss the matter with his wife, since she was represented by counsel, so I sought the aid of the local justice of the peace. Squire Jesse Bates was a man short of stature but long of cunning. He had the black hair and fine features of his "black Irish" ancestors. He was a son of "Black Rob" Bates, one-time state legislator, progenitor of Knott County, and its first sheriff. Black Rob's son possessed in full measure all his father's guile.

Squire Bates was an important figure in Letcher County's Democratic politics (he would later serve as his party's county chairman), and it pained him to see Democrats at odds because of a botched attempt at adultery. He visited the plaintiff at her home one morning and implored her to have mercy on the misguided Lothario. The squire said that this was her husband's first misstep (she was skeptical), that in all likelihood the other woman had tempted him (she frowned), that he was a hard worker, earned high wages, and did not drink (to be sure, all solid assets in a husband), and that he had already been punished terribly—worse than in a lot of murder cases. When she looked at the ceiling and emitted gales of laughter, the squire saw the glimmer of approaching victory.

She poured Squire Bates a cup of coffee. "Tell him to come back home," she said. "The poor idiot has suffered enough."

I collected a handsome fee for arranging this happy ending. The divorce action was dismissed. The Buick was repaired. There was no more playing around. The squire was remembered kindly at election time because of the constructive nature of his intervention. And, most happily of all, the truck driver took his wife and Big Mack and moved away, lifting a cloud of perpetual danger from my client's head. Thereafter, so far as I know, his life was a model of fidelity and rectitude. All was as before except for a network of long, thin scars on his face, limbs, and chest, and a slight limp in one leg.

5. Order in
the Court!

KENTUCKIANS HAVE LONG demonstrated a penchant for shooting one another. As I write this, there is beside me a newspaper that details these tidings: a dauntless Kentucky mother has shot her son three times because he tried to break in on her. A loving young woman has shot her gentleman friend because he stepped on her toe. In Harlan County numerous shots were exchanged in a dispute over the ownership of an old, abandoned car. Tomorrow there will be similar accounts, as there were yesterday and a hundred years ago.

Irvin S. Cobb, the Paducah humorist-author-actor, wrote that when he was a reporter behind the German lines early in the First World War, he was at a marked disadvantage compared to his hosts when it came to concealing his trepidation. The Germans had endured prolonged bombardments from enemy artillery whereas Cobb had been under fire only "a few times in school elections back home in McCracken County."

The English historian Arnold Toynbee wrote that the Appalachian people had "lapsed into barbarism," a charge one and all mountaineers hastened to deny. He wrote from the record accumulated in newspaper files, books, and court records, whereas we thundered back out of injured pride and self-righteous indignation.

Shooting up churches seems to be coming into vogue. The mother of Martin Luther King, Jr., was gunned down as she played the organ; recently in La Puente, California, a man killed one worshiper and wounded two others. It seems that the rest of the nation is adopting Appalachian gunmanship just as it has adopted the region's country music. Toynbee had feared that Appalachia would barbarize America, and that America would barbarize the world.

Shelby Elam of Lexington used to regale gatherings with his tales about growing up wild in Magoffin County. He told about a crowd of hardshell Baptists gathered on a peaceful Sabbath at a little church on Licking River. The preacher warmed up the congregation with a number of hymns, then started his sermon. A few minutes later his son entered with a pretty girl who had jilted a former suitor in his favor. The jilted swain followed them in and sat down across the aisle. He leaned over and called the preacher's offspring a son of a bitch, whereupon the one so insulted jumped up, pulled a pistol, and shot the offender through the heart. The victim's brother was at the back, lounging against the door jamb. Quick as a flash he drew his trusty revolver and slew his brother's killer. The preacher thereupon shot him. This wound eventually proved fatal, but not before the dying man got off another shot that wounded the preacher in the leg. I asked Shelby what happened after that. He said, "Church broke up!"

The general election of November 8, 1921, seems to have been especially hard on the good, law abiding people of Breathitt County. The *Courier-Journal* reported the next day that eight people were shot to death in election incidents at Clay Hole precinct. It seems that the right of a good old lady to vote in the school election was challenged, and this led to an altercation. The old woman ran away, but the men fought it out. First, though, the ballot box was seized and emptied into the nearby creek.

The day was unusually hard on the large and honorable Combs clan. Three of the dead were Combses, as were a few of the wounded. George MacIntosh shot Cleveland Combs. Attacking like an enraged panther, Mrs. Combs took away MacIntosh's pistol, and killed him with it. Another man, Lloyd Napier, was killed from ambush before he got to the polls. That afternoon the clerk of the election was shot at Simpson precinct. On election eve a man was killed at Spring Fork precinct. In lesser election outbreaks one person was killed in Knott County, two died in

Estill County, and a Logan County banker was shot after he attacked a poll watcher with his walking stick. The total slain in matters related to that year's election numbered fourteen.

Historically Kentuckians have not restricted themselves to seeing that elections are properly conducted. They have always displayed a keen desire to celebrate Christmas. Rejoicing became so merry on Christmas Day in 1900 that to list the dead required three days. The *Courier-Journal* casualty notices showed two dead at Mayfield, three dead in Letcher, two killed at London, two in Clay, one at Williamsburg, one at Middlesboro, a thirteen-year-old boy fatally wounded at Irvine, a man "shot through the heart" at Pineville, one killed at Hopkinsville, one at Stanford, and one killed at Bumpus Mills. John A. Robinson was ambushed and slain at Warsaw while visiting the grave of his mother. A general shoot-out involving fifteen men occurred at Louisa. In Clay County the home of T.T. Garrard was guarded by thirty-five armed men after his son was murdered. In all, the festivities brought twenty-two dead and seven wounded.

Sometimes fireworks break out in a courtroom under the stern and dignified visage of a circuit judge. In the circuit courtroom of the old courthouse at Jackson a large round indentation could be seen in the plaster just behind the witness's chair. It came there in this way: a young man was being tried for killing a neighbor of about the same age. The victim's mother sat on the front row of benches listening intently to the accounts of witnesses. As the defendant was testifying, the woman jumped to her feet and yelled, "I've heard enough of these damned lies!" She drew a pistol from her handbag and shot the defendant "straight through the heart." That was the end of the trial, but the dent in the plaster lasted until the courthouse was demolished.

Nor has killing within courtrooms gone completely out of fashion to this day. On September 25, 1977, in Knott County District Court an aggrieved litigant shot the two defendants to death. The suit involved $391.

My old friend—and sometime nemesis—Attorney W.A. Daugherty of Pikeville told me many stories about dramatic

trials in which he participated. He was present on March 14,
1912, when strong, violent men turned guns on a state court
and, within a few fiery seconds, virtually destroyed it. This
carnage at Hillsville in Carroll County, Virginia, was probably
the most dramatically-violent incident in the bloody history of
southern Appalachia. Describing the events of that horrible
morning forty years later, Daugherty's voice sank almost to a
whisper. Never before or after did he experience anything that
affected him so deeply.

In the fifty years after Appomattox, central Appalachia was
wracked by more than a score of interfamily wars. Scores were
shot to death, and widows and orphans multiplied. Houses were
burned, courthouses were torched, law officers were slain, and
not a few judges were slaughtered. But the "Hillsville massacre"
appears to have been an isolated incident unrelated to any of
these feuds. The people involved "just got mad" and short tempers led to a slaughter. The incident is fraught with lessons, one
of which is that if men find reasons for going about armed, they
will eventually find cause to use the arms, to their own ruin and
the great injury of society.

Sidna Allen was fifty years old in 1912. He was a man of
considerable substance in back-country Carroll County. He operated a farm and prosperous crossroads store. He lived in an
impressive eight-room house with an expensive slate roof. He
had a net worth of at least forty thousand dollars, a goodly sum
in 1912, and he owed no debts. He had done some traveling, to
Alaska to prospect for gold, and to Hawaii. A progressive fellow,
he had fitted out his house with a windmill to pump the water
from the well and an acetylene generator to provide gas for
lighting.

Sidna's brother Floyd, also a man of substance for his time
and place, had a reputation for both courage and integrity. In
1911 when a policeman was needed for the New River section of
the county, Circuit Judge T.L. Massie appointed Floyd to the
post. A third brother, Jasper "Jack" Allen, was a busy stock
drover and also dealt in hardwoods for the North Carolina
furniture industry. Clearly, these brothers were not slack-jawed
killers, but they were thorough-going mountaineers with all the
unpredictability that suggests.

The three brothers had a couple of handsome nephews born to their sister. Wesley and Sidney Edwards were sturdy, tall, straight young men twenty and twenty-two years old respectively. One Sunday they decided to attend a Primitive Baptist church service a few miles from their own neighborhood. Out of this simple act grew the "Hillsville massacre." Four young men of their own age saw them as competition for the pretty girls of the precinct and attempted to run them out of the county. Edwardses are said to be better at fighting than running, and a mighty tumult ensued. As a result, warrants were issued for the Edwards boys accusing them of disturbing religious worship. They fled to nearby Mount Airy, North Carolina, where they found jobs in a granite quarry.

These youthful fugitives from a minor misdemeanor charge seem to have aroused deep feelings among the Carroll County authorities. Dexter Goad, the circuit court clerk, obtained a new warrant for their arrest and sent two sheriff's deputies to North Carolina with directions to bring back Wesley and Sidney. Acting in another state where they had no lawful power, the deputies handcuffed their prisoners, bound them in their saddles, and returned to Hillsville by a road that led past the home of their uncle Floyd. When he saw his "own flesh and blood handcuffed and roped," he demanded that they be released to his custody. He promised to get the boys a bath and a shave, fresh clothes, and a good night's sleep. He was a law officer himself and would have them in the courtroom at eight the next morning. The two deputies brusquely rejected his proposal.

In those days blood kinship ties were exceedingly important. The idea of his nephews—the fruit of his sister's womb and almost as dear to him as his own sons—being conducted in chains, downcast and bedraggled, to the common jail aroused the fighting ire of Floyd Allen. Suddenly the roller-coaster ride to disaster sped up. Floyd drew his pistols and disarmed the officers, castigating them for "kidnapping" his nephews. He took away their rifles and broke their stocks. Then he bade them be gone, saying his nephews would see them in court on the following day.

The next morning the courthouse buzzed with indignation against Floyd and his nephews. A jury was empaneled and the nephews were tried. Both were convicted, with Wesley receiving a sixty-day jail sentence and Sidney receiving thirty days. They served their sentences and were released in time for Floyd's trial for illegally and violently releasing them from "the custody of officers having them lawfully in their charge."

When the day of that trial arrived, the courtroom was packed. On the bench was Judge T.L. Massie, the same jurist who had appointed Floyd a county policeman only six months earlier. Attorney E.W. Bolen sat as counsel for the defendant. The prosecuting attorney for the Commonwealth of Virginia was William Foster. The deputy sheriff who served the court was Lewis Webb. Dexter Goad sat at his raised desk to record the proceedings. In a section set aside for them sat prospective jurors. The onlookers were lawyers waiting for announcements in other proceedings, relatives and friends of the two outraged deputies, witnesses who had been summoned in various proceedings, and numerous relatives of Floyd Allen—his son Claud, his brother Sidna, his brother Jasper's son Friel, and Sidney and Wesley Edwards.

The courtroom was heavy with suspense, and, as it turned out, pistols. The favorite handgun was a long-barrelled .45, but there was a goodly scattering of .38-calibre Smith and Wessons. Clerk Goad carried a .38 automatic.

A jury was selected and the trial began. The five witnesses told their stories and were cross-examined. Instructions on the law were read by the court. The prosecuting and defense lawyers made their arguments. The twelve jurors retired to their room for deliberations. After a short time the court was adjourned until eight the next morning.

When the court was called to order on the following day, the crowd had thinned somewhat. Mr. Daugherty had arranged for a postponement of his case and was preparing to leave for his Pikeville office. Nearby sat a young woman, Bessie Ayres, who had been summoned as a witness in another pending case. All the officers were at their respective posts. Scattered about were Floyd Allen's relatives.

Within an hour the jury filed back into the courtroom with foreman Augustus Fowler clutching a verdict written on the back of the instruction sheet. It was handed up to Clerk Dexter

Goad who, with appropriate solemnity read: "We the jury do agree and find the defendant, Floyd Allen, guilty as charged, and fix his sentence at one year in the penitentiary."

A profound silence fell on the courtroom. From one end to the other the hush was complete. It was broken when tall, dignified defense lawyer Bolen rose and moved the court to grant an appeal. The motion was sustained. The lawyer then moved the court to allow the present bail bond to remain in effect pending the appeal. This motion was overruled. The judge declared that a new bond would have to be executed and approved. Floyd Allen whispered to Bolen that he could not produce the necessary bondsmen until the next morning. The attorney relayed this fact to the court who then ruled, "The defendant will be in the custody of the sheriff until such bondsmen appear and the bail bond has been approved. Sheriff, take charge of the prisoner!" The sheriff turned and took a step or two toward the defendant. Floyd, however, declared in a violent voice, "Gentlemen, I just ain't goin'!"

Precisely what happened next was never agreed on by the numerous witnesses who testified in the trials of the Hillsville defendants. There were seven trials altogether and the record of their proceedings is vast. The details may be in doubt, but the final consequences are certain.

A large pistol, loaded with a black-powder charge, boomed and Judge Massie slumped in his swivel chair, a little puff of dust rising from his coat lapel. Pistols then roared from the northwest corner, where Floyd Allen's relatives were mainly concentrated. Sheriff Lewis Webb fell as he had stood, his hand outstretched to take hold of the defendant's arm. He had a toothpick between his teeth and died so quickly that it never fell from his mouth. Commonwealth Attorney Foster was riddled as if by a machine gun. Jury Foreman Fowler was shot through the heart and hit the floor a corpse. Clerk Dexter Goad tugged his automatic from its holster and shot Floyd Allen in the leg. Floyd returned fire and the two battled it out until Goad's pistol jammed and he fled to an anteroom to remove the stuck cartridge case and reload. In this exchange a bullet struck the innocent bystander Bessie Ayres, wounding her fatally. Goad sustained a wound in his cheek and neck that cost him a tooth and broke his collar button. Another juror named Crane was shot twice, once in the back and once in the leg.

The accuracy and volume of the gunfire is awesome. It lasted less than a minute and there were few misses. The judge was struck by three bullets and the rail in front of him was shattered. The sheriff went down with five bullet holes in him. There were six in the prosecuting attorney, dropping him so suddenly that the book he was clasping under his arm was still securely in place when his body was picked up. A juror named Early testified that he escaped from the courtroom and was shot at from a window of the courthouse by someone who yelled, "There is a damned rascal. I will get him, too!"

Mr. Daugherty sat through all this with the self-possession of an old soldier who knows that to move when bullets are flying is to draw them to oneself. He said several young men were standing on benches in the back of the room firing like Custer's cavalrymen at the Little Big Horn. I asked him what he was thinking at that tempestuous moment. He replied with an earnestness that eliminated all doubt. "Why, I wished to God I had stayed at home!"

The Commonwealth of Virginia and the Baldwin-Felts Detective Agency hunted down all who were charged in the massacre. Two of the defendants, Floyd Allen and his son Claud, were convicted of the murder of Commonwealth Attorney Foster and were put to death in the state's electric chair on March 28, 1913. Friel Allen drew a sentence of eighteen years' imprisonment. Sidna Allen was sentenced to thirty-five years and was pardoned on May 29, 1926. (During his imprisonment he learned cabinet-making, including patterned inlays. One of his tables contained 75,000 pieces of inlaid wood and was referred to by a Virginia newspaper as an "eighth wonder of the world." The inlays were so precisely fitted as to be scarcely detectable by finger tips.) Wesley Edwards was sentenced to serve twenty-seven years. Jasper "Jack" Allen, the last of the three original Allen brothers, was shot to death on March 18, 1916, in a fracas in North Carolina.

Mr. Daugherty remembered Floyd, Sidna, and Jasper Allen as men of sterling character in the matter of personal honesty. "I would have felt perfectly safe to leave every dollar I own with one of them. He would have protected it with his life and returned it on request. They did not drink, and were good to their wives and children. Their trouble was their pride. They could not abide a personal affront. They would kill you in a second over some little matter most people wouldn't remember two minutes."

Pride goeth before a fall.

Many other Kentucky public officials have faced blazing guns. The task of protecting defendants until their trial has come and passed has sometimes proved impossible. A judge's adverse ruling has frequently been taken as a personal offense that inspired homicide. Even the state's chief executive has not been immune. When William O. Goebel was mortally wounded on January 30, 1900, by a rifleman firing from the office of the secretary of state, he became—and remains—the only American governor to be murdered while in office. The life of a judge of the Kentucky Court of Appeals (then the Commonwealth's highest tribunal) was snuffed out in 1876. Judge John M. Elliott was walking on a street in Frankfort when a disgruntled litigant emptied a double-barrel shotgun into his chest.

The county seat of Leslie County was named for a judge who was executed by kinsmen of a man he had sentenced to the penitentiary. In Jackson, county seat of Breathitt, Judge J.W. Burnett was gunned down in 1878 during a bail-bond hearing. In 1903, in the same town, the United States Commissioner for the Eastern District of Kentucky was slain by a shot fired from the courthouse. Across the street a few years later, County Judge James Hargis was killed at his store by his son. In Clay County the county attorney was captured on a public road and compelled to kneel, then shot to death by Jim Howard, the man who later slew Goebel. On June 10, 1899, a defendant, "Bad Tom" Baker, was killed while under guard by a company of militia men armed with Krag-Jorgensen rifles and a Gatling gun. The shot came from the home of the sheriff.

Most bizarre of all was the indignity inflicted on Circuit Judge William Pearl when he went to McKee, seat of newly-created Jackson County, to hold the circuit court's first session.

The place was crowded by people who had come to see the judge. Everyone had brought a dog or two, and the animals got into a vicious fight. They knocked over the judge's chair and fought in a scrambling, snarling mass on top of him. The men took up the cause of their battling canines, pulled their pistols, and began to shoot. Two men were shot to death and several others were wounded. The scratched and battered judge, his suit in tatters, fled for haven elsewhere.

At the trial of a murder case in Letcher in 1930 the judge ordered the sheriff to search all persons coming into the courtroom and not to allow anyone to enter who carried a gun. Each pistol given up for the day was identified by writing the owner's name on a slip of paper which was rolled up and placed in the barrel. The huge, heavy revolvers, mostly .44 and .45 calibre, filled two wooden banana crates.

During a proceeding about thirty years ago in the Clay Circuit Court my co-counsel revealed an enormous .45 revolver with a six-inch barrel lying discreetly in his open briefcase under the day's issue of the *Courier-Journal*. When I asked him whether he always carried that mammoth weapon to court he replied, "Hell, yes. If I have to shoot some son of a bitch, I don't want to have to shoot him more than once!" Once with that weapon would have sufficed.

Judges face many hazards in a land that teems with highly dangerous and heavily armed people. Their rulings inevitably incur enmities. About twenty years ago most judges began wearing judicial robes that are supposed to symbolize the dignity and solemnity of their office. Not a few of them also use the robe to conceal a holstered pistol. Within easy reach, it may enable His Honor to shoot back in self defense and in defense of his high office if an aggrieved party to a lawsuit resorts to violence.

Some hazards faced by Kentucky judges are even more difficult to deal with than an adversary's bullets. Judge Sam Ward described a pit into which he stumbled while holding court at Hyden. There was a local character named Couch who was known far and wide as Dirty Beard. This man, like the judge, was a dedicated Republican. His main failings lay in the infrequency with which he washed his whiskers and his habit of distilling moonshine whiskey. The latter practice caused Dirty Beard to be indicted by a grand jury on a charge of "making and selling untaxed whiskey in violation of the statutes in such cases made and provided."

Now all the county officials esteemed Dirty Beard as a pearl of great price and importuned the judge to save him from the consequences of his mighty crime. The judge advised them to tell Dirty Beard to come to court and ask for a continuance to the next term. After a continuance or two, the case could be quietly dismissed. "Tell him to bring me a good reason for putting off the trial," the judge counseled them.

Judge Ward supposed that when *Commonwealth* v. *Couch* was called by the clerk, Dirty Beard would announce that some catastrophe had befallen him—a misfortune so great that he had been prevented from preparing his defense—his wife was dying of an advanced disease, a child was suffering from some morbid ailment, the defendant had just risen from bed after a prolonged bout with pneumonia. These or any of a dozen similar excuses would have sufficed. The judge would have pondered his plight and recognized that to order the case tried would impose an injustice and hardship of a kind no citizen of a democratic society should be compelled to endure. But Couch was unlettered and uncomprehending. His courthouse friends had given him the message without advising him as to particulars. Thus when the case was read out from the docket, Dirty Beard stood up at the back of the courtroom. The judge solemnly admonished him to come forward. With imposing dignity he demanded, "What says the defendant? Are you ready for trial?"

Dirty Beard smiled pleasantly and replied, "Right by your foot, judge! Right by your foot!"

Judge Ward glanced down at the floor of the elevated bench. There he beheld a large shoe box. He used the toe of his shoe to shove aside the lid, revealing a half-gallon fruit jar filled with Dirty Beard's best straight-corn moonshine whiskey. Judge Ward said that he almost fell out of his chair.

A kindly lawyer who understood the circumstances stood up at that juncture and recited a list of misfortunes that had be-

fallen Mr. Couch. The case was continued, and Dirty Beard
escaped the wrath of the law.

And what became of the whiskey? "I gave half of it to the
lawyer and kept the rest for myself!" the judge declared.

The ways of the law are hard.

6. The Little Kingdom

IN 1912 OR THEREABOUTS the South-East Coal Company built a mining town in Letcher County, a mile or so above the confluence of Boone Creek and the North Fork of the Kentucky River. Today the community is dilapidated and unsightly, but in those far-off days of coal-boom euphoria the "miners' cottages" gleamed with fresh white and yellow paint, the coal tipple unceasingly poured coal into railroad cars, and the commissary was stocked to overflowing with all things dear to the hearts of American workingmen and their families. The town was called Seco, an acronym of the corporation's name. The company was founded by Henry LaViers, a Welsh coal miner who had immigrated to America with little more than ambition and a willingness to work. At the peak of a successful career that had seen him rise from a Pennsylvania pick miner to a successful mining tycoon, he was proud of his new town, his workers, and the profitable balance sheets his bookkeepers turned out each month. He was proud, too, of the little hospital that stood opposite the commissary.

Seen against today's glistening health-care facilities it was a pathetic thing, but when it was new, it was one of the county's marvels. It was built of wood and contained a kitchen, ten rooms for patients, and an operating room. It was highly inflammable and it is amazing that it stood a half century without burning to ashes and incinerating its patients. The people of the coal fields thought it was entirely adequate, and within its pine walls were treated hundreds of injured miners and sick people from miles around. Here, too, were born dozens of young Kentuckians who in later years would swell the ranks of the United Mine Workers of America, become, in a few cases, successful coal operators, and, in many other instances, join the great migration of Kentucky hill people into Indiana, Ohio, and Michigan.

In 1917 Henry LaViers recruited to the hospital a new graduate of the University of Louisville Medical School. His name was Benjamin Franklin Wright and he had been born and had grown up on a rough mountain farm where Seco now sprawled over creek bottoms and around hillsides. His father had been killed in one of the bloody wars that disgraced Kentucky in the forty years after Appomattox, and the young physician had overcome mighty odds to make it through medical school. But make it he did and even took some additional studies in surgery. When he moved into the Seco hospital he was regarded as "a mighty knowing young man."

The late Dr. Barnett Owen of Louisville, one of Kentucky's most skillful surgeons, told me in 1946 that he had taught courses in orthopedic surgery when Doc Wright was a medical student at the University of Louisville. He told me this story about Doc. A few weeks after the new doctor brought his new diploma to the new hospital at Seco, a terrible trainwreck occurred. Late on a spring afternoon a black hostler in the Neon yards undertook to clean the firebox of a steam locomotive by shaking the cinders out into an ash pit. He inadvertently released the brake and the engine leaped into motion, ramming a fuel car. The giant engine roared out of the yards pushing the fuel car and rumbled onto the main line headed down the Kentucky River toward Louisville and points beyond. A steel monster, vibrant with steam and unimpeded except by the fuel car, the locomotive rapidly gained speed and momentum. Suddenly it rounded a bend and confronted an L&N passenger train, complete with Pullman cars, churning its innocent way toward Neon and the Consolidation Coal Company's hotels at McRoberts. The engineer applied his brakes and sounded a terrified wail with his steam whistle. The miscreant hostler rolled out of the cab down a bank to the Kentucky River. He escaped into the woods and was never located, though a dozen wrathful lynching parties scoured the woods for him in subsequent days.

The two locomotives struck head-on, crumpling the intervening fuel tender. According to Dr. Owen, the carnage was terrible. The fireman on the uptrain was instantly scalded to death by escaping steam. Both engines derailed, carrying with them all the other cars. People were flung about chaotically and without warning. The bodies, ricocheting inside the steel and wood compartments, suffered fractures of every type—skull, arm, leg, pelvis, and rib. The effects in the foremost car were especially devastating. In those days of racial segregation a car designated for blacks was placed just behind the fuel car. This old, outmoded wooden "nigger car" as it was called, shattered into splinters. Twenty of the twenty-five passengers who died in that accident were in that car.

As soon as the L&N headquarters learned of the catastrophe, it assembled a fast special train, rounded up a team of surgeons (including Dr. Owen), physicians, anesthesiologists, and nurses, even a couple of embalmers, cleared the tracks of all other traffic, and sent the rescue train hurtling toward the mining hamlet. The train carried hastily-loaded operating tables, medicines, surgical implements, and a load of coffins.

Dr. Owen said that when they arrived at about 4:00 A.M. they found all the lights in the village burning brightly. Dr. Wright and his nurses had drafted several capable young camp women, and had begun operating on a big scale. Several crushed limbs had been amputated before doctors from Neon, Whitesburg, and Jenkins could arrive to aid Dr. Wright. Their combined efforts provided succor for the suffering and broken humanity. When the Louisville delegation arrived, "Young Wright was issuing orders like a German field marshal to the other doctors and their nurses." Dr. Owen declared that little remained to be done except to embalm the dead, arrange for burial of the amputated limbs, and make the injured comfortable on the trip to Louisville hospitals.

The L&N sent Dr. Wright a check for two thousand dollars (more than a fully-qualified school teacher would have earned in three eight-month terms). The paymaster was directed to distribute twenty-dollar gold coins as appreciation tokens to the camp women who had assisted him so competently and humanely. This event gave Wright a reputation that lasted unshaken to his death in 1969. He would become known to the farthest limits of the county, and whether liked or loathed, he would be called "Doc" Wright. And he would be involved in political scraps and scrapes throughout those forty-two years.

Seco and its twin town of Millstone, a short distance away, had been organized into an independent school district, and Doc promptly ran for the office of school trustee. Doc's father had died in the "Wright-Reynolds war," and the numerous members of the Reynolds tribe fought him tooth and nail. Doc won anyway, and thereafter his medical office was a political center where local intrigues were plotted morning, noon, and night. Doc had scant interest in political affairs beyond the county border, but he wanted to run everything inside those limits.

He subsequently gained county office as a representative in the state legislature and as county judge. He was county chairman of the Democratic party for a while, and in 1949 was elected to the county board of education. In due time he defeated all hostile members of the board and reconstituted it with people he liked to call "sensible men." He assumed the board chairmanship, got rid of the superintendent, and installed his brother-in-law in that post. Doc was then in a position to set up a more or less typical Kentucky political barony comparable to the historic Carter machine that ruled Monroe County, the Turner dynasty that reigned for nearly forty years in Breathitt County, and the McLaughlan organization that held sway in Jefferson. The Wright machine in Letcher was, like these and many others, a little kingdom where decades passed amid iron-fisted rule punctuated by the hubbub of occasional rebellions and suppressions.

Doc's rule depended on several factors: he possessed the kind of solid influence with one governor after another that enabled him to get roads built in the county and to choose the communities that would receive them. He controlled the school board with its construction jobs and patronage. He chose the state employees within the county who would handle public assistance agencies, supervise prison parolees, and work at road maintenance. His relatives or friends held virtually all public offices. It is understandable, then, that the governor—and several of them "served under Doc" when it came to affairs in Letcher County—often called to clear a wide range of matters with this backwoods overlord.

Doc's local prominence was illustrated during the Korean War. A less-than-brilliant Letcher Countian had been summoned to Huntington, West Virginia, for his Selective Service examination. In the course of his labors one of the examining physicians developed a doubt that the lad was bright enough to die for his country. He decided to test the prospective draftee: "Who is president of the United States?" The swain blinked. "Do you know who runs this country?" the doctor continued. "Shore I do," the youth shot back. "Well, who is it then?" demanded the medicine man. "Why it's old Doc Wright—everybody knows that!" came the reply.

During his long rule Doc demonstrated vast sagacity. He knew the laws that regulated school boards and set the qualifications of members. One such law prohibits a board member from directly or indirectly selling anything to the school system. Doc loved to see a compatriot violate this rule in some petty fashion, perhaps with vending machines for soft drinks or a sack or two of farm-grown potatoes sold to a school lunch room. Doc would keep a record of the incident and, if the offender subsequently became "obstreperous" (a favorite term with Doc), he would persuade the attorney general to authorize a suit to remove the offender and have him disqualified from ever again holding the office. During his long reign Doc successfully "cast out" (another favorite expression) two board members and two duly-employed but "ungrateful" school superintendents.

Doc could do these things because he had the ear of the state Court of Appeals and, except for the Willis and Chandler administrations, was warmly regarded by a string of governors, partly because he generously contributed to candidates and campaigns. But he did not use his own money. Doc extended invitations to all "the boys," and their wives and girlfriends to donate to the warchest of the upcoming struggle. They came alone and in pairs and trios, poor workers with crumpled ten-dollar bills, and the wealthy and well-placed with packets of cash. Doc expressed his gratitude for their generosity and jotted down the names of all who gave. But at Frankfort these donors were never mentioned. In presenting the benefactions Doc would remark, "I have brought a little donation to help out in the campaign. We can't win a war without ammunition!" Thus Doc reaped a generous return on the investments of others.

The coal fields teem with people who are disabled or sick, or who think they are, or say they think they are. Whatever their status—disabled, neurotic, or outright malingerers—they had to undergo examinations by a screening physician designated by the Department of Welfare (now quaintly rechristened the Department for Human Resources). Quite naturally Doc was appointed to perform this task for all cases that arose within the county. In election years—and in Kentucky every year is an election year—Doc liked to schedule as many examinations as possible a week or two before the electorate marched to the polls. Many of the impaired who swarmed his premises on these days were being reexamined to determine whether the condition had worsened or improved since the last examination. Each examinee understood that his fate hung by a thread and that his economic welfare depended on Doc.

The examination usually consisted of the claimant's opening his mouth and saying "ah" a few times, and baring his chest to a thorough examination by a stethoscope. While this was underway, Doc would give the patient a detailed rundown on the slate of candidates in the impending contest, including a discussion of their virtues. There was also a treatment of the shortcomings of opposing candidates and why a victory on their part would bring evil days to the county and state.

Needless to say, these sessions produced dramatic effects in the precincts. Virtually all applicants for state aid came across handsomely, and those who failed to cooperate at the polls were reported to the public assistance agencies as being "quite healthy." There were very few of the latter.

In 1953 when I was running for the state legislature, Doc invited me to sit in on one of these sessions. He said it would give me some exposure with the "welfare elements." He introduced me to each sufferer at the beginning of the examination, and then enumerated my supposed virtues: I was a war veteran and an uncommonly good lawyer, and as I was sympathetic to the poor and disadvantaged, I was much needed in Frankfort. When released from the stethoscope, the hopeful claimant to total and permanent disability invariably wrung my hand and vowed to do everything within his power for me. Before yelling "next" to the bereft waiting patiently outside, Doc would smile at me and wink.

Early in his political career Doc was an ally of the wily A.B. "Happy" Chandler, but after Chandler became governor in 1935, there was an acrimonious parting. Doc explained that the rupture was caused by Happy's ingratitude, but Chandler had another explanation. Pointing out that every two-mule team consists of a lead mule and a trail mule, Happy said, "Doc fell out with me because he wanted to be the lead mule. I was the lead mule, and Doc wouldn't heel in and be a trail mule." No clearer explanation was possible.

I must emphasize that Dr. Wright's turbulent career as a political boss was a secondary concern with him. He was an excellent physician and a fine surgeon whose reputation was deservedly well-established in professional circles in Lexington and Louisville. He was an uncanny diagnostician. After serving a few months in Italy during World War II, I suffered a series of debilitating episodes of extreme chills and fevers. I was subjected to blood tests and treated with antibiotics, but to no avail. Finally, I gave up on the new doctors with their fancy machines and dragged myself off to Doc's long-antiquated facility. He gave me a quick but thorough examination and declared, "You have all the classic symptoms of malaria." He prescribed quinine and I promptly recovered. For more than two decades since then I have gone nowhere without a vial of this essential medicine. Doc sniffed, "These young doctors spend so much time with their lab tests that they overlook the patient. The patient should be thoroughly examined for symptoms at the start, but now they go at it the other way around. First the tests and then the examination. I don't like it!"

But this venture into the colorful career of a coal camp doctor is only a preface to a story Doc told me a year or two before his death. It is a tale of youth and love, and exemplifies the strange and unexpected turns by which destiny sometimes thwarts and frustrates both.

One bright September day we were driving to a coal property Wright was thinking of selling. He was in a merry mood because he had thwarted and humbled a political adversary with what he called a "master stroke," another of his favorite expressions. He was almost gleeful as he recounted the adventures that had befallen him a half-century earlier when he was a vibrant eighteen-year-old youth.

In 1892 when he was born, the upper Kentucky was mighty hardscrabble country. In that age before railroads, farming was the mainstay of life, supplemented by rafting out saw logs on spring tides, and selling dried ginseng and sometimes a few hides or bags of feathers. Money was exceedingly scarce before national debts made it abundant and cheap. Doc and his brothers distinguished themselves in their years of manhood as physicians and businessmen, even though they had grown up poor and without the economic and social support systems that have so vastly multiplied laziness and irresponsibility in recent decades.

It was the season of golden summer and by dint of much effort the physician-to-be had acquired enough money to buy himself a new suit, shirt, and hat from Sears, Roebuck and Company. He was very proud of all his splendor, but was most proud of his new high-top, black patent leather shoes. They were a perfect fit and when he got into his crisp, fresh attire, he felt mighty handsome. The cause of all this effort was a lissome, blond, blue-eyed girl whose father owned broad bottomlands amid his thousand or more hillside acres. Doc was "struck on" the girl and intended to do something about it. He didn't know what, precisely, but he was strong-willed and inventive. He had met her only once, at a square dance a few weeks before, and being immediately smitten hastily expended all his small hoard on suitable garments. Unfortunately for his incubating schemes, the damsel's father had gotten wind of their chance meeting and the mutual interest they had shown in one another. He sternly forbade his daughter to see young Wright again because he was destitute and his people were notorious feudists. He planned to marry her in due time to someone with far better prospects. This, of course, only increased the young woman's interest in seeing the forbidden youth, and she managed to get a message to him that she would spend the coming Saturday night at the home of a cousin. They met at the cousin's house, he in his impressive new garments and she so beautiful in face and form that he scarcely noticed what she wore.

She tempted him with a plan a more cautious man would have feared to consider. Her parents' home was an old fashioned L-shaped, two-story frame house of a kind once common among prosperous Kentucky farmers. It was painted white with blue trim, and its sheet tin roof made the rough split shingles of his neighbors' homes appear humble indeed. The house stood near the county road, and her upstairs room was easily reached by an outside stairway that led up from the porch—a strange arrangement, but a feature prevalent across the Appalachians and in much of the rural south. Her parents went to bed early and slept soundly. Ben Wright could silently creep up the steps, the waiting maid would open the door, and they could spend the following hours in ways that have beguiled young men and women since Adam and Eve.

A signal was arranged. She would set a burning coal-oil lamp in her window. He was to wait in the darkness by the roadside until she blew out the lamp. This would signal that her parents were asleep and he could safely creep up the stairs.

Darkness found young Ben crouched down by the road near the gate to the yard. The two watchdogs came to investigate and barked a time or two, but he rubbed their heads and they soon wandered back to their sleeping place under the porch. Dusk turned to darkness. The stars came out, but the moon was only a sliver and gave no light. On needles and pins with anxiety he watched the glowing lamp for what seemed an age. Then to his vast pleasure the flame disappeared. Ben rose and crept through the gate. He paused. He realized that he could not climb those hollow wooden steps in his stiff new shoes without making a frightful clatter. He must ascend to his love in only his socks. He stooped, untied and removed the shoes, and neatly set them together on the flat top of the foot-thick locust gate post from where he could retrieve them easily when he departed. Moments later his beautiful friend's door was opened for him and he took her graceful form into his arms.

In later years Doc experienced the delights of three marriages, (and the tumults of two divorces), but the most glorious of all his nights was the one he spent with this beauty while her protective father snored below. The hours passed blissfully with never a thought for the morrow, but his happiness ended when he heard heavy feet hit the floor below and the clangor of an iron poker stirring the ashes in a wood-burning cook stove. Dawn was creeping upon the land as a cock crowed in a nearby tree. The girl twisted in his arms and whispered, "Leave, Ben, quick! If he finds you here he'll shoot you for sure and he'll beat me to death!"

In a trice he stuffed his shirt into his trousers, flung his coat over his shoulder, and crept with stockinged feet down the steps. Ben heard the man of the house speaking to his wife in a room beyond the kitchen and leaped across the porch onto the lawn. At this sudden movement the dogs sprang from under the house and, barking and growling ferociously, chased the interloper across the yard and down the road. So hotly was he pursued and so eager was he to escape the wrath of an outraged sire that he completely forgot about his magnificent new shoes, sitting damp with summer dew atop the post. His pace was quickened by the farmer's yells of "Stop Thief!" The dogs harried him for a hundred yards until he cooled their enthusiasm with some well-directed rocks.

Ben was used to walking barefooted on mountain trails, so that posed no hardship. It occurred to him, however, that his neighbors would think it passing strange to see a young man, dressed up like a city dude in a classy black suit, white shirt, and blue tie, walking the rutted county road in limp socks. So he took to the timbered hills and made his way home unseen by meddlesome neighbors.

Naturally, his mother and brothers were puzzled by his mid-morning arrival in such dishabille but he answered no questions and told all alike to mind their own business. He pondered the delights of the evening, dampened somewhat by loss of his esteemed shoes.

A few days later Ben was at a country store near the mouth of Millstone Creek. Numerous idlers lounged on the porch, among them the burly father of Ben's ladyfriend. The merchant, who hated to see people in the neighborhood order goods from the catalogue houses, remarked on the handsome new shoes that encased the farmer's feet. Ben's nemesis cleared his throat and spat some tobacco juice. "The strangest thing happened with these here shoes the other mornin'. Just at the break of day my dogs started raisin' hell and I run out to see what was goin' on. Somebody was runnin' down the road as fast as he could go with my dogs a-barkin' and a-growlin' at him. He disappeared in a second, fast as a shot. When I went out to see if he might have stole somethin' and run off with it, I found these shoes all polished up a-settin' on top of my gate post. Somebody had brought these here shoes in my exact size and set them up there fer me, and then run off. It must have been somebody who knowed me and liked me a lot. I can't figure it out!"

Then after a long puzzled silence he added, "It had to be somebody who liked me because he got me the exact right size. A stranger wouldn't have done that."

He and the crowd gave up on that riddle. Ben went sadly home after casting a last lingering look at his gleaming shoes, now lost beyond hope of recovery. Lost, too, was the girl. Within months she married a school teacher and they moved to Oklahoma.

Doc told me another story about his misspent youth, a story that cast him in the unlikely role of what is now called an abused child. A farmer named Quiller Bentley had many acres of bottomland planted to corn. It was a rainy spring and the corn was choked with weeds. Bentley sent out the word that on Monday morning all comers would be hired to help him rescue his crop. He would pay men fifty cents for a day's work, and boys would be given a quarter. Each worker should bring his own hoe. Dinner would be free, all they could eat. "Dinner" in those days meant a huge meal in the middle of the day.

Doc, thirteen at the time, qualified for a much-needed quarter and arrived at daybreak with his hoe. Two huge mules dragged plows along the furrows between the rows, and the men and boys struggled to keep up with them, chopping out every weed and raking fresh dirt around each corn hill. Hour after hour they toiled, the boys compelled to stay abreast of the men, though they were only half as big and drew but half the pay. At ten, when the sun began to blister necks and sear shoulders through cotton shirts, they rested for fifteen minutes while the water bucket made its rounds. Then the labor resumed without let or stay until the clangor of an iron dinner bell announced that dinner time had arrived.

The weary men and boys rested a few minutes in the shade of a big Milam apple tree, then filed to the sumptuously-laid table. They devoured corn pone, fried pork and potatoes, beans, pickles, plenty of butter and biscuits, and strong hot coffee. Twenty minutes after leaving the table, they renewed their attack on the weeds. When the last row of corn was clean and weedless, they dragged their weary way to the house. There the mistress of the place paid each his quarter or half-dollar.

Doc said he was too exhausted to walk home. He stretched out on the rough boards of the porch, his joints aching and his stomach as hollow as if he had eaten nothing for days. From the kitchen came the heavenly fragrance of frying spring chicken, the aroma of boiling coffee, the smell of tender biscuits browning gently in the oven of a wood-burning stove. The boy yearned with all his heart to get at the table.

After an age "old lady Bentley" yelled, "Come and git it!" The men of the house moved away from the porch, but Doc remained on the floor, limp and empty. Presently the good woman appeared at the door and spoke to him, "Ben, honey, would you like to eat supper with us?" Doc sat up, a hopeful "yes" exuding from every pore. At the table he gobbled food like a famished man— chicken, fried potatoes, beans, corn bread, biscuits, cold milk, hot coffee, golden butter. When he left the table, it was dark but he had regained the strength to walk the two miles to his home. He thanked Mrs. Bentley for the good food, picked up his hoe and started for the gate. Before he got out of the yard, however, the clear, confident, commanding voice of his hostess called to him. "Ben," she asked, "ain't you fergot somethin'?"

"I reckon not," he replied. "All I brought was my hoe." But she persisted, "Now think about it. Ain't you fergot something?"

Then his heart fell like a stone plunging into a well. "Ben, honey," she unctuously chided, "you fergot to pay me for your supper!"

"How much is it?" he asked in a feeble whisper. "Why it's just a quarter, that's all," she smiled with her palm outstretched.

The boy drew the coin from his ragged trousers and dropped it into her hand. She went behind the stove and he heard it clink as it fell amid other coins.

Doc said that was the hardest day's work he ever did. It lasted more than twelve hours, and all he acquired for it was the food he ate for his supper. Doc never forgot the episode, which helped to harden and temper him as fire tempers steel.

Incidentally, Mrs. Bentley later sent two of her own sons through medical schools. When she died, a large cast iron kettle behind the stove was found to contain $58,000 in the lawful coinage of the United States.

Destiny deals with human beings in strange ways. No passer-by meeting that exhausted boy on the rutted county road could have dreamed that one day he would be a skilled physician, the political czar of his county, a man who knew governors, congressmen, and United States senators on a first-name basis, sat as a delegate in at least one presidential nominating convention, and possessed enough worldly wealth to enjoy complete financial security. Yet such ascents from poverty to prominence and power are commonplace in American history. I often wonder what early-life influences the incomparable Lincoln might have described had he survived to write an autobiography.

At his political zenith Dr. Wright caused a new word to be coined. It never entered the dictionaries, but it deserves to be remembered because it reflects so well the flavor and character of rural Kentucky politics. In a state consisting of only forty thousand square miles but divided into 120 small counties, innumerable divisions and factions inevitably arose. In the little kingdoms, political wars erupted over every conceivable public act, acrimony became the language of politics, vengeance seeking became more important than public service, and a political stratagem had to be rank indeed to shock the public conscience. It was in this atmosphere that Dr. Wright and scores of fellow-spirits ruled the counties and fashioned public policies from the mid 1930s to about 1970. It was a colorful era in the state's politics, and remarkable progress was made despite the chaotic infighting and position-seeking that characterized that dramatic time and its public characters.

The word was coined by "Big Bill" Adams, a devout Republican who made his way into the legislature for a term or two despite Doc's vehement opposition. In the midst of a campaign, one of the Republicans made a political speech in which he proposed to push certain policies if elevated to the office he so earnestly desired. Big Bill thought the proposal a bad one and unworthy of the Grand Old Party. "You are talking Docism," he accused the speaker.

Though Doc died in 1969 his influence has not wholly passed. As this is written his nephew, Charlie Wright, is serving his tenth four-year term as Letcher County court clerk, and has high prospects of being elected a few more times. His is one of the longest tenures in the state's history and may eventually equal that of Jesse Combs, who held the office in Perry County for fifty-three years from 1820 to 1873. His grandson then succeeded him.

Doc told me about an interesting and unusual facet of his ancestry, and one to which he attributed much importance. During the Civil War, General James Garfield (later president of the United States) took an army of Ohio unionists up the Big Sandy to disperse one or two regiments of ragged mountaineers who were attempting to hold the region for the Confederacy. Garfield's soldiers camped for a time where the town of Jenkins now sprawls beneath the Pound Gap of the Pine Mountain. Among the Ohio troops was a German immigrant, a young Jew named Wilhelm Luntz. Disenchanted with campaigning and the prospect of being dismembered by Minié balls, he deserted. A few miles away the charms of a young mountain woman named Wright caught his eye. She and the fugitive soldier became great friends and took up their abode together in a deserted log cabin that stood in a mountain cove. When Luntz later returned to Cincinnati to make his fortune, he left her with a little boy whom she raised under the name of William Luntz Wright. The child became Dr. Wright's father. Thus Dr. Wright, a dyed-in-the-wool mountaineer, was one-fourth Jewish. The Jewish grandfather became a wealthy man dealing in cattle, logs, lumber, leather, and medicinal plants brought down out of the southern mountains for sale in the Cincinnati markets. He acquired a Victorian-era brick house with the towers, turrets, domes, bay windows and gargoyles typical of the style, where he was visited from time to time by mountain drovers and commodity dealers who came to settle their accounts. Seen in this grand setting he was considered a wealthy man. Doc was proud of this part of his ancestry. "Everything about a man is in his chromosomes," he said. "If it hadn't been for him, I might have been a little pointy head."

After Doc's death his only surviving son had his name legally changed to Luntz. "I don't want to sail under false colors," he explained.

Doc also had some strong blood from his mother's side. Through her he was a great-nephew of "Bad John" Wright, the fabled mountain feudist-gunman-peace officer who was accredited by balladeers and storytellers with having shot to death twenty-two adversaries. From the same source he was great-nephew also to "Baby" Bates, the "biggest man in the world," the largest soldier who served in the Confederate Army, who, with his giantess wife, produced the largest baby known to have been born alive.

There were giants in the earth in those days.

7. Politics Kentucky Style

NEARLY ALL LAWYERS DABBLE in politics at one time or another. The electorate labors under a delusion that lawyers are uniquely qualified to make laws and hold public offices, whereas Thomas Jefferson warned people to elect their poets and sages. He thought barristers are made cynical by their early exposure to the dark and sinister underside of life. Be that as it may, there is a chronic shortage of both poets and sages in the Bluegrass state so that, of necessity, people turn to lawyers for their legislators and administrators. All judges must be lawyers. Then there are the county and commonwealth attorneys and their assistants. Consequently courthouses are filled with diligent-looking, blue-suited, briefcase-toting counselors on their way to deal with the weighty affairs entrusted to them by their clients or by the voters.

Americans are litigious people and keep lawyers busy, mostly with trivial matters. Rare is the lawyer who has not entertained political ambitions or, more likely, ventured into the political waters in the hope of securing legal fees to be dispensed by his cronies. Consequently, many law offices are centers of political intrigue where candidates are groomed, campaign funds are solicited and dispensed, strategies are mapped, and political speeches and platforms are drafted.

Most lawyers come from political families and have heard much talk of elections and political spoils. Thus their professional lives may be extensions and fulfillments of early political ambitions. This was true to some extent in my own case, though by my mid-thirties I had concluded that politics was too costly a game and should be abandoned so some money could be saved.

The Bell County town of Middlesboro near Cumberland Gap was built by an English corporation in the 1890s. Among the "furriners" who came there was a Scot from Glasgow, Cro Carr. My grandfather admired him so much that when my father was born on December 9, 1892, he was given the unusual Gaelic name of Cro Carr Caudill.

My father lost his left arm in an accident at a Consolidation Coal Company tipple during the bitterly cold winter of 1917. In 1925, and again in 1929, he was elected county court clerk of Letcher County as a Democrat, and that at a time when three-fourths of the voters in the county were hard-to-sway Republicans. Letcher County lies at the headwaters of the Big Sandy, Kentucky, and Cumberland rivers and is walled in by the Pine and Big Black mountains. Its granitic adherence to the Grand Old Party was a living legacy of "the War." In the history of the county to that time few Democrats had managed to poll a majority for any county-wide office.

My father was inventive and played on the mountaineer's tendency to sympathize with the unfortunate and the handicapped. He hired an old woodcarver named Ed Thomas to turn out hundreds of wooden statuettes. The figure, painted white, was a crow with an outstretched right wing. The left wing was missing, a poignant reminder to coal miners, moonshiners, farmers, and housewives that he could not fly or scratch like other birds. The message sank home and the candidate was elected and reelected as the "one-winged white crow." He was aided, too, by the support of Consol, which announced a favored slate of candidates for each election and viewed as "ungrateful" and "undependable" anyone within its towns who wavered in support of that ticket. Few wavered.

In later years he successfully managed political campaigns at the local level for several state-wide candidates, including Tom Rhea's race for governor in 1935 and Alben Barkley's campaign for reelection to the Senate in 1938. John Y. Brown's race against A.B. Chandler in 1942 was a more limited success. Brown challenged the immensely popular "Happy" Chandler and was crushed, losing 118 counties out of 120. My father, continuing his life-long feud with Happy, managed to squeeze out a lead of a few dozen votes for Brown in Letcher County. Chandler was elected lieutenant-governor, governor, United States senator, and governor again, but Letcher was one of the few counties he never carried in a primary. One-winged Cro and his friends were able to deprive their old adversary of the satisfaction that would have come from a clean sweep.

Major Cornett, brother of the inimitable and indefatigable Lilley, told me how they carried Sugar Grove precinct for Cro in the 1929 general election. My father's opponent was a good woman named Amanda Gibson, a staunch Republican and a widely-known stenographer and court reporter. Sugar Grove was truly a Republican bastion—not a single Democrat voted in the precinct. It looked hopeless for Cro when the polls opened at six o'clock.

Lilley and Major were Republicans, but they were not for Mrs. Gibson. Cro had done them a personal favor which they thought deserved a favor in return. To that end they were prepared to carry Sugar Grove for him—a difficult feat requiring "ticket scratching." As we shall see, however, it could be arranged.

A few days before the election the brothers told Cro that the voters were thirsty and wanted a drink. "Go up the creek to the next house," Lilley counseled, "and buy us two gallons of good moonshine. Bring it back as soon as you can and then get gone. The very sight of a Democrat will make these Republicans mad. We will take care of the rest."

Within an hour the white lightning had been bought and delivered. Full of grim forebodings that he faced a debacle at Sugar Grove and that he had wasted the eight dollars invested in the illegal whiskey, Cro despaired that the voters would get the moonshine and Amanda would get the votes.

As it turned out, his pessimism was baseless. When the sheet-steel ballot box for Sugar Grove was opened at the courthouse on the following day, it was discovered that nearly all the ballots showed crossovers in his favor. He had carried the precinct at the rate of four to one. When he saw his benefactors again, he asked for an explanation of his splendid victory. As Major and Lilley described it, the operation was simplicity itself.

The brothers sent word to the arriving voters that they were "treating for Mandy Gibson" in a thicket behind the school-house. Their lips panting for the whiskey and eager to cast a vote for the party's female standard bearer, the electorate arrived at the hiding place. There were the jugs filled with whiskey foaming to a magnificent bead each time a jug was lifted or shaken. But the expectations of these drinking voters were not realized. Lilley and Major gave each a gruff explanation. "This whiskey belongs to Mandy Gibson and we're treatin' people for her so she can beat Cro Caudill. But you don't git any 'cause we know you are already fer her and will vote fer her whether you git a dram or not!" This invariably made the voter "a sight on earth mad," and he rushed away to vent his indignation on the unfortunate Amanda. "The way we managed it," Major recalled, "your dad carried the precinct and we got to keep all the liquor and drink it ourselves."

In Kentucky, elections are only as honest as circumstances require. Even when balloting has been fair and square, the count is often rigged. Many a slip occurs between the closing of the polls and the official certifying of the result.

An elderly gentleman from Democrat Precinct on Rock House Creek told me how Cro once carried that citadel of Republicanism. This precinct too was without a single Democratic voter. All four election officers were stout-hearted members of the GOP. The precinct took its name from the local post office, which was authorized in the days of Woodrow Wilson. The postmaster-general had complied with the residents' petition that a post office be established to serve the needs of the people in that wild and remote area, then piled an everlasting vexation on their heads—every letter they mailed carried as a postmark the name of the political party they detested.

My aged client was a precinct election officer on the day when Lilley and Major were "treating fer Mandy" in Sugar Grove. The turnout in Democrat Precinct was heavy. When the last vote was in the box, the four election officers, went to my client's home for supper, proudly carrying the box in their midst as a display of their awesome official responsibility. The weather turned cold and rainy as they ate, and they decided to spend the night under the same roof and deliver the box to the county election commis-

sioners on the following day. In the meantime it would be vig-
ilantly guarded by four Republicans—two for the GOP and two
for the Democrats.

They sat before a dancing coal fire; other people in the household drifted off to bed. The four guardians of the public franchise
talked about religion, the hereafter, and the Holy Bible. One of
them remembered that Saint Paul was opposed to women being
preachers and had written that they should remain silent. The
implications of this were pondered and discussed. Then one of
them mentioned Gibson, who was not remaining silent but was
in politics trying to get elected county court clerk. This, it was
perceived, was against scripture. It would "go agin' " the Bible
to elect her, and yet Democrat had done precisely that. God, it
appeared, needed a little help, so they provided it. By unan-
imous consent the box was jimmied open. The ballots were
examined and, as expected, nearly all were marked for the
straight Republican ticket. The biblically-inspired election officers then marked all but two of them to show a vote for Cro
Carr Caudill. The altered ballots were returned to the box, and
in due time it arrived at the courthouse, where its contents were
counted and certified. The precinct went Republican except for
Mrs. Gibson, who received a mere two votes.

My father had been dead ten years when I heard this story.
My informant told me that the other three election officers had
long since passed on and that neither my father nor anyone else
had ever been told about their session with the ballots. "Every
man in that precinct claimed that he and his wife had cast them
two votes for Mandy Gibson," my friend chuckled. "We might
have done wrong," he mused, "but I don't think so. How could a
woman 'remain silent' if she was a public officer? She would
have to speak up every day there in the courthouse. It would
be part of her job, and a sin she would have to commit. No, I still
think we done the right thing for her and the whole county!"

When I asked him about the book, chapter, and verse on
which he and his associates had relied that night, he said he
didn't know. He had never actually read the passage himself, but
had "heerd tell" many times that it was there all right,
"somewhere between the covers of that Good Book."

Emerson "Doc" Beauchamp (pronouced Beecham) of Logan County was a consummate politician who lived and breathed Democratic party politics. The Logan County machine had been abuilding for a long time under the indefatigable leadership of Thomas S. Rhea. When Beauchamp inherited leadership of the organization, he was already a major voice in the party's councils. At the state level he held several sensitive posts where deft political maneuvering could consolidate and enlarge power and influence; he was commissioner of rural highways, lieutenant-governor, and commissioner of agriculture. Beauchamp, like Rhea and many other practitioners from Kentucky's western reaches, won elections through an incomparable combination of quick wit, sleepless devotion to the cause, and unfailing courtesy. The Logan County machine rolled to victory year after year for generations. For all practical purposes the machine embraced everybody in the county and no one complained about any questionable practices except maybe outraged editors from Louisville and Lexington. These sometimes stirred up little waves of indignation in other sections of the state, but Logan Countians ignored such momentary flare-ups and proceeded as before. Prosecuting attorneys, judges, and prospective jurors— all who could have taken action against the machine—were part of it and could be counted on to protect it from attack from within and without.

While Beauchamp was lieutenant-governor, he came to Whitesburg on a political mission. I was a member of the legislature and he came by my office to discuss some problem of mutual interest. That day the *Courier-Journal* had carried a story about nefarious political practices in Logan County, and referred to reports that hundreds of dead people had voted at the last election. The tombstones of the deceased voters were located and photographed. These pictures were published beside photographs of poll signature sheets showing that the departed brethren had appeared, received ballots as in the days of old, and cast their votes. The article raised grave doubts about the ability of these dead Democrats to exercise a lawful franchise and suggested that numerous persons were guilty of election frauds.

Doc and I discussed the article and he denied nothing. His comment pretty well summed up the position of Kentuckians in all times and counties when caught voting the numerous dead whose names continue to linger on the voter lists. "What Mr. Bingham [editor and publisher of the *Courier-Journal*] doesn't realize is that we knew all those dead people the paper has written about. We know they were all good Democrats who would have liked to keep on voting for their friends if they could have. We were just carrying out their wishes, and if we had died first they would have done the same for us." Then after a moment's reflection and a smile: "A man is not much of a Democrat if he won't help out a dead buddy!"

Kentucky's first absentee voting law was enacted during World War II for the benefit of service men and women. As fleshed out in later years it applied to all who were absent from their homes on election day—or expected to be. The out-migration that carried so many hill people to the North in the 1950s deposited vast aggregations of Kentucky voters in Detroit. Most continued for a long time to vote "back home" by absentee ballot, and their votes were often decisive. The Democrats were especially effective in garnering those ballots for their slate.

In one election in which I was the nominee for the legislature, the Democratic slate sent a "tried and true" emissary to Michigan to canvass those transplanted "briar hoppers." Lists compiled, he went from house to house persuading the men and women to sign the necessary applications for absentee ballots. When the ballots began to arrive at the mail slots a few days later he returned with "a hired notary public" and saw that they were marked and sealed in envelopes as required by the statutes, and that the affidavits of the voters were signed and notarized. He then supplied postage and dropped the envelopes in the mail.

When the official tabulation began, apprehension spread among the Democrats. The opposing "tickets" were neck and neck as several precincts were reported. As concern deepened, our emissary to Detroit came by to comfort us. "Don't worry," he said, "just wait till you hear from Hamtramck!"

When the absentee ballot box was opened our spirits were refreshed. It contained 482 Democratic "straights" to 11 for the Republicans.

Some of the founding fathers were dubious of democracy.

Alexander Hamilton wrote, "Give the votes to the people who have no property and they will sell them to the rich who will be able to buy them." Coal, tobacco, and whiskey are Kentucky's largest industries, but buying votes is a major one also; it probably eclipses the other three on election days. Politicians recognize this and discuss it among themselves with complete candor. It is rarely talked about publicly, however, for fear of injuring the sensibilities of the "good people."

Richard P. "Dick" Moloney of Lexington would have made Kentucky a great and progressive governor, but his religion precluded his election. He was a Roman Catholic and, as the 1960 presidential race demonstrated, not even the Kennedy millions could induce a majority of Kentuckians to vote for a "popist."

Moloney was a powerful figure in the state senate for eight years, serving as president pro-tem during most of that time. He gave up his senate seat to run for the house, where he was promptly elected majority floor leader. His was the most consistently progressive voice in the state's government, supporting school improvement, resource conservation, and equal rights for blacks and women. He was unbeatable in Lexington, the state's most prosperous city, where Irish Catholic influence was strong. When I asked him why he had left the more prestigious and influential senate for the tumultuous house, he explained it in terms of money.

"My senate district takes in several of the old 'silk-stocking areas' of Lexington. The people live in good homes and are old money. By contrast, my house district includes what remains of Irish Town, and the rest is mostly black. It costs me about $5 for each vote and I like the savings. I can finance my campaign for the house out of my own money and that leaves my hands free after the election. A senate race requires financing from outside sources—and obligates me to the satchel men." That is the way an honest man dealt with politics' unquenchable thirst for money, a thirst that led to Watergate, the corrupting of an entire administration, and the resignation of an American president.

"Doc" Wright was Letcher County's political potentate for

decades. As his personal attorney for twenty years I had many frank political discussions with him. I once asked him to tell me the principal element of his winning formula. His reply was blunt and forthright: "I don't pay much attention to the good people among the voters. They will generally split about even between the candidates. I go after the trash vote. The man who gets the trash vote wins the election!"

Like other successful politicians, Doc was supremely contemptuous of the public. "The remarkable thing about the common people," he once remarked, "is that they are so God-damned common."

He knew that, in the main, people are gullible, greedy, and selfish, and he used rumors and innuendo with devastating effect. His corps of a half-dozen trusted aides could carry a ruinous suspicion to every precinct within a couple of days, and few candidates struck by his "ducks"—as he termed them—ever recovered.

In one hotly-contested election Doc was determined to defeat an incumbent. The official's wife was a gentle, harmless soul whose sole occupation was being a housewife. She was almost never seen in or about the courthouse. A few days before the election the doctor's spokesmen spread out over the county repeating the following scenario with slight variations several dozen times. Stopping at a coal-camp commissary, where a little group of men were idling away the hours, pleasantries were exchanged and the henchman bought everyone a Coca-Cola. He inquired about the election in general, then about the official's race in particular. He didn't have much interest in the races this year, he observed. As to the incumbent, he was a mighty good man. Hard to beat. Had too much money, probably, not to win. Then he left them something to discuss among themselves and to tell others.

"Don't quote me on anything," he said in the most confidential of tones, "but it is entirely possible—just between you and me—that he has his wife on the county payroll at $20,000 a year. She doesn't do a thing for the public, almost never sets foot in the courthouse, as a matter of fact. It is certainly something that will bear looking into because the people ought to know. It is the public's money she is drawing."

A moment later he was gone, and within a day or two this scandalous nepotism was the talk of the county. No one "looked into" the matter but everyone talked about it. From possibility it turned to probability, then to certainty: the man was paying his wife $20,000 of the taxpayers' dollars each year for absolutely nothing! No wonder he drove a new car and looked prosperous!

The incumbent vehemently denied the story. In fact, he swore it was a lie, and said so in a speech on local radio. But the half-dozen voices went back to the precincts and countered his denials. "If there is nothing to the report, why is he going to so much trouble to deny it? A man with a good record doesn't have to deny anything—his record speaks for itself. Besides, where there is smoke there is fire!"

The abused public servant went down to defeat. Doc said his ducks had nibbled him to death.

Successful political campaigns require enormous sums of money. When Bert Combs was a candidate for governor in 1959, former Governor and United States Senator Earle Clements came down from Washington to give him a helping hand. Clements was a tireless fund raiser and in due time turned his attention to Letcher County and his old ally. One day he called the doctor's home and was told that he was at my office attending to a legal matter. When the call reached my desk, I exchanged a few pleasantries with Senator Clements and handed the phone to the board chairman. The exchange that followed was unforgettable.

The two marvelous old veterans of the political wars asked most courteously after wives and loved ones. There were inquiries about mutual friends, and chuckles over bygone elections. Then Clements got down to the business of money, and my client's expression changed to noncommittal attention. I could not hear the senator's end of the conversation, but it was not difficult to reconstruct. The campaign was going well, Combs was comfortably ahead, but money was essential. Letcher had always been generous and the state organization had never failed to reciprocate in the political game of mutual back-scratching. Combs's election would enable him to help his friends in many ways, to their continuing profit. Right now, though, there was need for money—about twenty thousand dollars to be exact—and the inevitable question was, "Can we count on you and our other good friends to come through and help us out to that extent?"

Doc Wright's answer summed up the dilemma of the political contributor who wants to gain both goodwill and victory. It could have come only from a position of entrenched and confident power, and it capped a conversation between two men who understood one another perfectly. "Now, Earle, I will tell you how it is with this money raising. We can get the money together for you; there is no doubt about that. But here is the trouble. When we collect the money, we'll keep some of it; that's human nature. Then, whoever comes up from Frankfort to get it will steal some of it on the way back. When it gets to state headquarters, somebody will have to keep it and be responsible for it, and he will steal a little. When we get ready to finance the precincts here, the money will be sent back, and whoever brings it will steal some more on the way. When it gets here we will steal some of it again, and then when the election comes we'll run short."

Then Doc proposed: "Let's do it this way, Earle. You fellows look after the rest of the state and we'll take care of Letcher County and make sure Combs carries it by a good solid margin. We'll finance this county and not ask for a cent from state headquarters. That way the Letcher County Democrats will keep their money at home and just steal from each other!"

Alben W. Barkley was the nimblest political gymnast I have ever met or had an opportunity to observe. In a long political career he served as commonwealth attorney in his native Mc-Cracken County, United States representative, senator, and majority leader, and vice-president under Harry Truman. He once admonished me that in politics any discussion of issues is dangerous. "The public is not interested in issues and is bored by a discussion of them. My policy is to entertain the people by telling them jokes and stories, and to educate them by raising hell with the Republican party."

In 1938, when I was fifteen, I went with my father to Campton in Wolfe County to hear Barkley address an immense gathering of mountaineers. They had poured in from the creeks and hollows of five or six counties, afoot, on mules, and in wagons, and in trucks and battered Fords. The New Deal work and welfare programs were supporting thousands of families, converting innumerable Republicans to "Roosevelt Democrats." After Barkley had been introduced as "the only American fit to sit at Franklin D. Roosevelt's desk if some misfortune befalls that God-sent man," he commenced the education of his enthralled listeners.

"Some people will tell you there is no real difference between the Republican party and the Democratic party, but I tell you there is not just *a* difference—there are many differences: The Republican party is the party of old, dilapidated schoolhouses and half-starved teachers. The Democratic party is the party of fine, consolidated schools like the new one the P.W.A. is building on this hill overlooking Campton. The Republicans yell 'balance the budget,' and let the people live in shacks and eat bread and a little gravy made with water and flour. The Democrats say 'sell a few bonds to the rich bankers'; then take the money and pay men to build roads and schools so they can have meat in their skillets again. The Republicans have never built a mile of road in Wolfe County since the county was created, but the Democrats have thirteen road projects underway at this very time!"

There was much more in the same vein, comparisons depicting Republicans as the dullest of laggards on the one hand and arch villains on the other, while the Democrats stood forth as the champions of progress and defenders of the common man at all times and places. Warming the hearts of his audience, he concluded, "When the Republicans are in office, the working man prays to God for a little bit to eat. When the Democrats are in, the working man thanks the Creator for the bountiful repast he has spread before him and is about to enjoy. Truly, my friends, the good Lord works in wondrous ways his marvels to perform!"

The happy Democrats clapped, hollered, and pounded one another on the back in transports of glee. Barkley shook hands with hundreds of them and was driven away, still waving his hat when the car rounded a bend.

Some time later the great man was scheduled to speak again, this time in Clay County, where Republican support was so entrenched that infants imbibed their political beliefs with their mothers' milk. The New Deal had made some converts there and in adjoining Leslie County, but in the main the people still adhered to the One True Faith. I wanted to see how Barkley would handle this challenge, so my father and I and a couple of friends made the three-hour trip to Manchester. The dusty little town was crowded, but when Barkley arrived the crowd was silent. The few Democrats the county could claim welcomed him and shook his hand, and when he came forward to speak, they alone applauded. The Republicans stood silently, their cheeks stuffed with Brown's Mule tobacco, from which frequent streams of ambeer were emitted.

As he had done at Campton, Barkley rose to the challenge without a trace of hesitation or doubt. He knew that Clay Countians had heard of his give-'em-hell speech at Campton, so he picked up where he had left off. "I am sure," he began, in the Barkleyan manner that was half roar and half ham acting, "you have heard that I made a speech at Campton and had harsh and unkind things to say about Republicans and their party. Well, I can't help what idle gossips who want to stir up trouble and discord say as they make their poisoned rounds, but I can tell you the truth about my good friends of the Grand Old Party.

"When I was a young man down in McCracken County, I got to feeling lonesome and in need of a wife. I started looking around for the right kind of girl and I met her one day at the county fair. I fell in love with her at first glance and made inquiries about her. I learned that her father was, among other things, a good farmer and the strongest Republican in all that part of Kentucky.

"As soon as I could arrange it, I made her acquaintance and, without delay, asked her to marry me. She refused at first but eventually agreed, and she has been my good wife now for many years. We have children and grandchildren and have never had a cross word in all this time."

He paused to assess the crowd, which was all attention. "Every night when I go to bed," he resumed, "she is there beside me, warm and sweet and tender. And each time I turn off the light and reach over in the darkness and pull her over to my side of the bed for a hug and kiss . . . [another pause, and then in a voice even the deaf must have heard], I say to myself, 'Thank God! Thank God for the Republicans!' "

My old friend Charlie Wright, Letcher's county court clerk since 1949, once told me how he had contrived to smooth the feathers of a disgruntled but locally-influential Democrat who, for some wholly baseless reason, had decided that Charlie was dishonest. Nothing had been effective in winning him over until the following idea occurred to Charlie. He waited until the disgruntled voter came in to renew his automobile license, and that evening went to his house. When he had been admitted, Charlie produced a quarter and a one-dollar bill. The clerk explained that he had discovered an error in the good man's payment. He had been charged a dollar and twenty-five cents too much. The discovery had caused the clerk deep anguish and he had come at once to make restitution. "Not for a hundred and twenty-five *thousand* dollars would I lose your respect and confidence!" Charlie averred. The man was deeply touched. He apologized for not having supported Charlie in previous elections. The next time around, Charlie said, "He electioneered all over the precinct for me, and worked at the polls all day. All it cost me," Charlie noted, "was a dollar and a quarter. Actually he hadn't been overcharged at all."

On a number of occasions I have been asked to write a political speech for a tongue-tied politician and have found it flattering to hear my prose resounding on television and radio. In 1956, for example, Earle Clements was running against Thruston Morton of Louisville for reelection to the United States Senate. Morton was well-known and popular in northern Kentucky, had the support of the *Courier Journal* and *Louisville Times,* was amply financed, and—most important—was on a ticket with Dwight Eisenhower. Not only was the Democratic party split into warring factions, but in a long political career Clements had accumulated many adversaries. He was in serious trouble.

As the campaign advanced Doc Wright decided that he would deliver an address for the good senator. He contacted the television station at Charleston, West Virginia, which broadcast to the homes of most Kentucky mountaineers, and bought fifteen minutes of prime time. He asked me to write a "hard, no-nonsense" speech about the Republicans and their shortcom-

ings, and assured me that I would be paid for my efforts out of
party funds. I took on the job with relish and was proud of the
double-spaced pages I delivered to him a couple of days later.

His appearance on television caught both camps by surprise.
The doctor began with a brief resume of his own years of public
service out of which had grown a strong dedication to ordinary
working men and women. He would speak, he said, from that
background and that dedication, directing his thoughts and
concerns to coal miners, loggers, school teachers, housewives,
and all the other men and women who live by their labor. There
followed ten minutes of direct frontal assault on the Republican
party as the party of the rich and uncaring. He scornfully called
Herbert Hoover the grand architect of the Great Depression,
and conjured up the awful days of the 1930s when a Democrat
named Franklin Delano Roosevelt arrived on the scene to save
the country from a Republican-engineered collapse into starvation and anarchy. He moved on through peace and war, acclaim-
ing the victories of the world-wide conflict as the natural results
of dynamic Democratic leadership in the White House and
Congress. In all of this Earle Clements had played a major part.

Now, slack times had come again. Doc described the coal-field
depression, the emigration that was rapidly depopulating whole
districts, and he exhorted all toilers to support Clements. "He is
your only logical choice," he declared. "The railroads, the power
companies, the coal companies—all the economic interests that
Franklin Roosevelt had to fight in order to get bread to your
tables—already own Morton!"

When Doc finished, the telephone calls were already lighting
up the switchboards as Democrats expressed their jubilant approval. The calls continued through much of the next day, and
whole carloads of Democrats drove to his office to voice approval
and pledge support. All this left the orator as proud as Punch.

The Republicans, however, were outraged. When I opened my
office the next morning, one of them was waiting for me. "I was
so mad," he said, "that I didn't sleep a wink." He was my client
on a regular basis and he wondered whether I might be persuaded to write a reply to that "scurrilous" speech. He knew I
was a Democrat, of course, but he nevertheless considered me
his kinsman. He felt that as a fair man, I would never approve of

such outrageous lies. "Old Doc claimed the Democrats have done all the good and the Republicans have done all the bad since the beginning of time. Why, God damn it, he might as well have accused us of inventing hell!" He assured me that I would be paid for my services. "Just add the fee to your charges in my lawsuit and no questions will be asked."

A mellow-voiced character was lined up to deliver the rebuttal and the time had already been contracted for. It was a slow time for lawyers, so I took a note pad in hand and went to work.

Three nights later mountain Democrats were scandalized by what they heard in their own living rooms. A young Republican took up Doc Wright's challenge and for fifteen frightful minutes laid on blow after dreadful blow. He was, he assured his listeners, a veteran of the Pacific war and had listened to Doc Wright's odious attack with disbelief and outrage. He and some of his war veteran friends were spending their own money to set the record straight.

The Democrats, he declared, were the party of war, and built prosperity on the blood of dead Americans. He called the roll. The war with Mexico was fought under a Democratic president. The Civil War began because Democratic governors and legislatures seceded from the Union, thereby declaring war on the United States. In 1898 Democrats in Congress declared war on Spain. In 1917 a Democratic president and Congress went to war against Germany, mixing in a foreign conflict of a kind George Washington had warned against. In 1941 a Democratic administration imposed an oil embargo against Japan, demanded that Japan end its war in China and then, after having done everything possible to goad the Japanese to war, retired from the scene and let a handful of Japs creep up and sink the United States Navy! After that calamity came the Democrat Truman and the Korean War.

These wars had cost the nation more than a million dead—young men in the prime of their lives. These wars had brought about wartime prosperity, it was true, but the wages and profits were blood money. Eisenhower knew war as no Democratic president had known it, as commander of the greatest and most successful fighting force in the country's history. The way to peace was with Eisenhower and Morton. The way to another war

somewhere in Asia was to elect a Democratic president and
Congress. They would find someone to fight somewhere because
that was the only way the war party knew to generate what they
called "good times."

The speaker had scarcely told his listeners good night when
my telephone rang. It was Doc Wright and his first words were,
"I have never been so God-damned mad in my life! I want you to
get to work immediately on an answer to that rascal's speech.
I'm going to reply on television, then have the tape run on all the
local radio stations in the mountain counties."

Doc's vehement rebuttal "set the record straight." His voice
was vibrant with indignation as he invoked patriotism—"the
love of country"—to shame this "so-called veteran and the party
that sponsored him." Yes, wars had been fought under the Democrats, but they were just and righteous conflicts. Jefferson was
the Democratic governor of Virginia and its Kentucky County
when the Revolution was fought for American independence.
The war with Mexico made Texas free and enlarged the United
States by a third. The war with Spain drove the oppressors out of
Cuba, a mere ninety miles from our doors. The first World War
saved European civilization and our own from the murderous
Hun. And World War II? It brought the rapacious Japanese to
their knees and closed Hitler's monstrous death camps. Korea
checked Stalin, "a tyrant worse than Genghis Khan." To question the moral rightness of these wars was to brand every patriot
who fought in them a dupe and a fool.

His speech rejuvenated the Democrats and left the Republicans foaming with rage. The doctor's counterthrust came too
late, however, for the GOP to return the blow except for a
number of hastily-devised spot announcements that went wide
of the mark. But a battle of the tapes at the local radio stations
persisted with unflagging zeal to the last hour.

On the day before the election I drove to Catlettsburg for a
court hearing. During the ride back, I heard my profundities
flying back and forth like balls from blunderbusses. At Catlettsburg I heard Doc Wright charge Hoover with "following policies
that starved women and children." A few miles farther along he
was accusing the Republicans of ruining all that FDR had accomplished and dragging the country "backward into the

darkness of another Depression." He referred to the president as "Eisenhoover." The station at Prestonsburg was castigating the "War Democrats and the only kind of prosperity they ever generate—the prosperity of blood, death, and heartbreak." From Hazard came Dr. Wright's description of "Kaiser Bill's atrocities" and Hitler's furnaces "where good decent people were turned into ashes for garden fertilizer." As I approached Whitesburg, I was warned by a Republican to be on the watch for "Democratic libels and lies." A few minutes later I learned that the "Democratic party will not let the Communists take over the world. The Republicans seem to be saying that freedom and the flag are not worth defending."

Neither my Democratic nor my Republican client ever divulged the authorship of these utterances. The doctor was too proud of the vitriol he had dumped on his adversaries to allow anyone to suspect that the words were not his own. The GOP was allowed to suppose that my client had concocted the acidulous assault on the "War Democrats." As for myself, I learned that it is great fun to write political speeches for both sides in a bitter, hard-fought campaign.

Probity did rule my pen on two occasions, however. A couple of students aspiring to become doctors of philosophy offered me handsome rewards to write their doctoral dissertations. The father of one laid ten one-hundred dollar bills on my desk as a retainer, the rest to be paid in cash when the work was finished. The proposition became almost irresistible when the candidate (who was eager to get away to a Kentucky-Tennessee basketball game) chimed in with, "You won't need to fool with the footnotes. I will get my girlfriend to go through the library and stick them in here and there." But still I did not yield. I have wondered many times who supplied the wisdom-packed lines that earned him that coveted certificate.

8. Buried Alive

COAL MINING IS THE MOST dangerous of the nation's major industries. A committee of the Harlan County Junior Chamber of Commerce reported that more than twelve hundred miners perished in the mines of that Kentucky county between 1912 and 1986. At the Lynch mine of United States Steel Corporation (whose motto was "Safety the First Consideration"), 180 died in the years 1919-1930. Between 1847 and 1977, 121,209 men and boys died in American pits. Of these, 702 were killed in major explosions in the month of December 1907.

The gigantic methane and coal-dust explosions cause dramatic stirrings among the purveyors of news and so are remembered longest. The greater number of mine deaths, however, come one or two at a time and are little noticed. A thick slab of slate or sandstone slips out of the top and crushes a workman to pulp. A miner fails to see a fellow workman and crushes him with a machine. The insulation on an electric wire erodes and a man is electrocuted when he touches it. On a strip mine a man is buried by fifty tons of rock that tumble from the top of a highwall. Insidiously over years coal dust, slate dust, and silica dust accumulate in a miner's lungs and he suffocates by slow degrees.

Despite determined efforts by labor unions, coal companies, and state and federal agencies to make the workings safe, death lurks wherever men mine coal.

In my years as a country lawyer I heard countless tales of close brushes with death. One that made an especially deep impression on my mind was related by a man about my own age who was working with his father when a slab "about a foot thick and bigger than a mattress" broke through roof supports onto the "old man." He said that when the dust settled, no part of his father could be seen.

He went for help, and mechanical jacks were used to lift the slab a foot or two from the floor. When a beam of light was pointed under the slate, "only the clothes and a greasy place" could be discerned. After the stone was broken up with sledge hammers and hauled away, the miner took a shovel and "scraped" the remains of his father off the mine floor and put them in a body bag improvised out of a piece of canvas brattice. It may be truly said that coal mining is not proper work for the faint-hearted.

Though I have had the good fortune never to work in a coal mine, I have had much second-hand experience with its hazards. My father's left arm was ground off in a tipple accident. My brother had a leg crushed in another tipple accident. An uncle died of pneumonia induced by inhaling "bad air" after an accident destroyed the mine's ventilation fans. Before machines did most of the labor in mines, armies of men worked underground, and regiments of the wounded could be seen on the streets of coal-field towns. Some were blind or one-eyed, others were one-armed, legless or on peg legs, on crutches or in wheel chairs. Men are still killed and maimed in mines, but machines now experience most of the mishaps.

Early in this century the states began enacting workmen's compensation laws. Before these laws were passed, the courts adhered to "the assumption of risk doctrine." This rule held that a miner knew the hazards of the trade when he accepted the job and therefore was entitled to no compensation for injuries sustained in the mine, unless the mine operator deliberately did something to cause the accident. The state's law provided a scale of payments for disabilities caused by "traumatic" injuries. Trauma was interpreted by the courts to mean a blow or striking—in other words, a sudden and violent injury. In those early days the notion of psychological injury or impairment had not worked its way into the law or the popular mentality. If a man claimed injury, he had to "show his scars."

The definition of trauma was extended to include psychologi-

cal blows, or blows to mind, nerves, and spirit in a case decided
by the Kentucky Court of Appeals in 1955. In that action the
state's highest court ruled that a man could be disabled or killed
by an experience that left no visible scar on body, head, or limb,
but was an invisible, damaging blow to his mind, spirit, psyche,
and self-confidence. Thus death or disability could ensue
though the worker had lost no drop of blood, no patch of skin, no
hair from his head.

The man whose misfortune brought about this historic extension of the law was a small, wiry miner named Worley Dickson.
He told me that he was a strong, able workman before a twenty-
six-hour misfortune befell him. After that, he said, "I have not
been any account for anything. I can't seem to gather my
thoughts and concentrate my mind to work. I'm jumpy all the
time, and can't get any rest out of my sleep. In the back of my
mind I keep hearin' rocks grind together, comin' closer and
closer to me, and I hear the rock under me a breakin' up and a
shiverin'. I never thought I was a coward, but I know now that I
am."

He went to work on February 14, 1950, as he had done on
similar mornings hundreds of times before. The small truck
mine in which he worked was on the Kona ridge, a few miles
from the headwater spring of the North Fork of the Kentucky
River. The operation was owned by two brothers, Henry and
Goebel Adams, and carried the resounding name of Fire Chief
Coal Company. It was one of hundreds spawned by the war effort
after Pearl Harbor. Mining equipment consisted of picks and
shovels, a drill or two, steel track rails and wooden ties, some
bank cars, and a few muddy shetland ponies to pull the loaded
cars from the coal face to the tipping horns above a rough
wooden hopper. Trucks backed up to the hopper several times a
day to carry the fuel to a railroad siding. These primitive mini-
mines have long since passed into history, but in the dozen or so
years after America went to war they added much to the country's industrial muscle. Hundreds of such works produced many
millions of tons of much-needed coal.

Worley Dickson lived beyond Pound Gap in Wise County,
Virginia. His son Paul and his son-in-law, Ernest Bryant, had
homes nearby and each day they drove twenty miles to work the

Adams mine. They and Dewey Rose were the inside men who daily set new timbers to secure the top, put up collar poles or timbers on the headings as the tunnel was driven ever deeper into the coal vein, drilled holes in the face of the coal, tamped explosives into them, and loosened the coal by a blasting process called "shooting from the solid," that is, without undercutting. They shoveled the coal into the cars which a driver conveyed to the tipple. The workplace was then cleaned up by loading the discarded slate and muck for hauling to the refuse dump. Then a few yards of steel rails were laid on black oak ties to bring the track close to the coal which would be worked the following day. In this way they worked a section of the mine, while other crews operated similarly in nearby sections.

They were working a coal vein known as the Elk Horn No. 3, a fuel renowned for its high quality and its sound, stable slate and sandstone top. When they had left their section at the end of the previous work day, their operation was in good shape—clean, well-timbered, and with heavy sawed white oak timbers collared to the face. The new track was in place and brattices were hung properly to direct the air from the ventilation fan into their work area. At the tipple they greeted other workers making ready for the new shift, then bent their heads and entered the main heading. As they walked the three hundred yards to make their cut, they felt a reassuring flow of cool air on their necks and shoulders. One of the owners, Henry Adams, was an experienced mining engineer, and he supervised a well-maintained mine. They anticipated an uneventful day's work in which each of them would earn at least twenty dollars, substantial pay for 1950.

The morning's work was without mishap and at least twenty tons of glittering Elk Horn coal was sent down the tracks to the outside. At a little past noon they met with their buddies (a corruption of the Welch mining term "buda" or friend) and ate dinner near the entrance where the flow of air was strong and fresh. After a short rest they made ready to finish the day's tasks.

But when they returned to the workplace off the end of the tunnel, they stopped dumbfounded. A rock "a little bigger than a bale of hay" had broken loose from the apparently solid top and now lay about two feet away from the coal face. The support timbers were unbroken and the collars appeared intact. They discussed the unexpected development and the task of cleaning up the fall and retimbering the room, no little vexed at this troublesome, costly, and unexpected development.

But scarcely had a moment passed when they were galvanized by the unmistakable snap and crackle of splintering roof timbers and the duller thump of breaking rock. The top was coming down in the main heading—the only tunnel that provided access to or escape from their work space, a room about twelve feet across and thirty feet deep. If work proceeded according to plan, the area would be extended day by day into a new lateral tunnel leading to the coal "bloom" on the outer edge of the hill. But that was prospective only. Now it was a dead end from which there was no escape. During the night the top had "worked", causing the block of stone to drop to the floor, and now the only escape route was being closed by a collapsing top in the heading.

They were like soldiers caught in the open by an unexpected barrage: they had to find shelter in a split second or die. The collar timbers extending from the tops of white oak posts on each side of the room were beginning to sag, with dirt sluicing down out of fissures that had not been there a minute before. Fueled by terror, Worley Dickson dove for the space behind the fallen rectangle of stone. He was not a large man and he shot between it and the coal face like a nimble fox. The flame of his lamp went out as he slid into the tiny space and drew up his knees to get his feet inside the space. Out of the corner of his eye he saw his son-in-law spring out of the room and, running close against the coal rib, flee past the descending top and out of his sight. Dewey Rose froze for an instant and was crushed by an avalanche of tumbling rock. The seven-inch sawed collars snapped like shotgun blasts, the white oak posts supporting them pulverized to splinters, and the roof rock plunged with a mind-numbing roar onto the block beside him. The falling rock smashed down like a stupendous fist, until the block held it about sixteen inches above the floor.

Dickson was in total darkness. He lay on his side with his knees drawn up. The bottom of his steel-toed shoe touched a shard of the fallen roof. When he moved his head, his cap was only inches from the same fall. He described the space as being like that under an overturned bathtub. He did not feel pain in any part of his body. Miraculously he had not sustained so much as a scratch or bruise. His heart thumped like an overworked piston engine and he was already soaked in the instantaneous sweat of terror.

From above he could hear the rustle and snap of sinking stone and soil as additional segments of the top settled into the void. Occasionally the mass would slip and become tighter from the increasing weight. The rubble seemed to sigh as it accepted the vast new pressures.

Bit by bit his pulse slowed and he undertook to assess his plight. What was his situation? How long could he last? Did he have a realistic hope for escape? When and how would death come to him?

The first fact he faced was that his little cell was about five-hundred feet in a straight line from the entry. The entry tunnel was strongly timbered with oak and hickory, and the fall had probably been localized at his working room and a few yards beyond. If the main heading had collapsed to the outside, his doom was sealed. Otherwise, men rallying to his rescue might be able to dig him out—but not for a long time and only if the rubble above him could be moved without bringing new collapses out of the guts of the mountain.

There were some pluses. In the first place, he would not suffocate. Fresh air was reaching him, which indicated that the main tunnel was intact with the fan still shoving air into it.

He thought about nourishment. His stomach was full. He had eaten a hearty workingman's dinner and would not starve for a long time. He had taken a long pull at his drinking water and so could endure the torture of thirst for some days. The temperature of the place was cool but not unbearably so. The overpowering problem was with blood circulation. How long could he live "scrootched up" without stretching his arms and legs? The question was enough to stir yearning for space, for movement, for straightening his elbows and knees, for twisting his neck, and getting the curve out of his spine. But movement was impossible. He had enough room for life, but just barely and only enough extra to move his head forward or back by an inch or two. No coffin could have gripped him more securely. He was a strong, healthy, uninjured husband and father—and he was buried alive!

And what of his son-in-law, Ernest Bryant? From what he had seen in that horrible second, there was a chance that his swift leaps close against the coal rib had carried him entirely beyond the limits of the fall. He might even now be reporting the accident, or he might lie only yards away beneath twenty tons of roof rubble. Dickson simply could not know. He could only hope and pray.

As to Dewey Rose there was no doubt. The roof fall had caught him in a deluge of rock and there was absolutely no possibility that he could have survived. His corpse lay about ten feet away, a paste of formless bone and flesh.

An age passed in darkness that was stygian and in silence that only the faint sigh of his breathing interrupted. His pocket watch had shattered in his leap for shelter so that he was deprived of even its faint ticking. He had some matches in a pocket but could not reach them to make a light. He lay on his right side with his nose close against the hard face of the Elk Horn coal. He detected the faint taste and smell of sulfur as tiny particles of the mineral settled on his lips and his nostrils. He closed his eyes to shield them from what he knew was a relentless rain of the microscopic grit. At the same time, he was seized by an overpowering need to sneeze. When they came, the sneezes reverberated and somewhere a post snapped, triggering a faint sifting of sand onto the rocks above him. An ankle began to itch but, study the problem as he might, he could devise no way of scratching it.

Amid these torments he found consolation. Thousands of coal miners lived in Letcher and surrounding counties. He knew that when the report of his misfortune spread, they would rally to his rescue. His fellow miners would not rest until he was brought out and the corpse of his friend had been recovered. The question was not whether they would come for him, but whether they would be able to devise and execute a rescue plan within the time limits imposed by his own capacity for survival.

After another age he thought he heard a noise, or at least the ghost of one. He could not identify it, but knew it was human. He drew in a deep breath and yelled, "Here I am! Here under the roof fall!" He supposed that men had come from the outside and were looking from a safe distance at the collapsed roof.

Then a sound sweeter than the music of harp or lyre came along the cracks and openings in the rubble. "Hush, men! Listen!" Then, "I'll be damned if he ain't hollerin' under that rock pile! Two railroad cars couldn't carry off them rocks but he's still a-hollerin' down under there!" More declarations followed, some of them no little profane.

Another age passed. Then the voice boomed again: "We've got to go now, Worley. We'll git help and dig ye out. It will take time and we have to have engineers. We'll bring Henry Adams back and plenty of men. We'll git ye out, now, so don't worry. How are ye fixed down there?"

Dickson yelled at the top of his lungs, "I'm scrootched up against the coal face with mighty little room. The top has settled and is steady. I'm a-layin' straight opposite the entry into th' room. I can't see and don't have any room, but I ain't hurt."

He paused for breath, then yelled, "Tell Dewey Rose's wife that he is dead. The rock fall hit square on top of him." Then, after resting a moment, he shouted, "Did Ernest Bryant get out past the fall? Is he alive?"

The voice came back. "Now, Worley, you stay quiet. Your son-in-law is okay. He didn't even get a scratch, and is carryin' timbers. Don't talk anymore. Save yer breath and strength so you can help us find ye when we get ready to dig ye out!" Then the stillness returned and silence engulfed him.

Somehow he slept, or maybe fainted.

In any event time passed and he abruptly sprang back to consciousness. Every joint in his body screamed for movement and he was overwhelmingly thirsty. Simultaneously the coffee and other fluids he had drunk hit him with an irresistible desire to urinate. But amid these torments and the darkness there was a sound. It was a jumble of noises and they were not distant. A rescue effort was afoot and many men were in the tunnel. First, they would have to retimber the approaches to his crypt, and then . . . ?

He lapsed into and out of sleep or stupor. Twice he talked with

a man who yelled at him from the edge of the rock pile, the voices
carrying along the voids between the slabs. He learned the
strategy of his rescue. "We are not goin' to move these rocks. It is
too dangerous to even try. We are goin' to drive a new tunnel into
the coal seam and come in behind you. We have fifty men at work
and the coal is really flyin'!"

At another time he talked to Ernest Bryant. "What time is
it?" he queried. "About six o'clock. You have been in there all
night," Bryant answered.

All night! The weariness, the tedium, the pain had, he supposed, taken up many days. When time cannot be measured,
when no sun moves across the sky and there are no bells to ring,
no meals to eat, no birds to sing, when existence is dark and
silent, there is no measurement of one's life. Long and short are
the same.

He tried to pray but was overcome by a sense of foreordina-
tion, as the old time Baptists say, a feeling that everything in life
is predestined. God, he thought, must have put me between
these rocks for a purpose. If he has a further purpose for me, he
will lift me out. Somehow it struck him as unseemly to pray to
God from such an ignominious and inconsequential situation.

Presently a new worry beset him. He heard a squeak a few
yards away, a sound that could have come from one rock riding
down hard upon another. But there was another possibility, and
it was terrifying. He had seen no rats in the mine, but he knew
that they often frequented such works, coming up onto the tree-
grown hills from the coal camps. If they were in the tunnels,
they would be drawn to the broken body of Dewey Rose. In that
event they would surely make their way to him and they would
find him helpless. Pale panic swept him as he imagined their
scurrying feet, their needle-like teeth tearing into his cheeks,
into his eyes. Then he forgot the ignominy of his circumstances
and prayed with as much fervor as a soul can muster.

The sounds increased to a continuous clink and rattle. They
were muffled sounds, and made remote by the rock, but they
were distinguishable. He could make no sense of the yells or the
distant rattle of tools, but his chilled blood was warmed by them.

But even as the rescue operations encouraged him, a new
discovery brought alarm. His fingers detected handfuls of sand

at the base of the rock behind which he sheltered. It had not been there before and a moment's consideration revealed its source. The sandstone was crumbling under the weight, its disintegration hastened by the drying circulating air. The stone was in a race against time and he would perish in the inevitable moment when it went to grit. Even as he realized this new peril the protecting slab shivered and a crack ran from its top to its bottom. Now his life hinged on two separate stones each about twenty-four inches across.

There followed another interval of unconsciousness which ended when he snapped awake to discover that his bladder had yielded to the inevitable. This humiliation swamped him with frustration and he huddled in despair.

In the hours of his confinement events elsewhere had moved rapidly. At least three score men had arrived within two hours of the accident, and as some tired others took up their tools. A rescue team from the State Department of Mines got to the scene at 10:00 A.M. The situation was assessed from every aspect. The first goal was to bring out Worley Dickson. Secondarily, Dewey Rose's remains must be retrieved. After securing the entry with additional roof supports, two crews went to work on the separate tasks, while a third whisked away accumulated coal and rubble.

The engineers ordered that the heading be redirected so that an extension would go beyond the ill-fated room. Then, leaving a coal pillar intact, they mined through the intervening deposit to a point just behind the rock fall. The coal cuts and all blasting were small, but followed one another in rapid succession. The new heading reached within a dozen feet of Dickson's dungeon more than a day after he was imprisoned. Extreme care was necessary from this point on. A miscalculated blast could kill him if it was too potent.

The next explosion was barely capable of cracking and loosening the coal barrier. As soon as the fan cleared the air, some attacked the coal with picks while others shoveled it back to the cars. Timbers were set and tightly cap-wedged against the top.

At this point the remaining coal weakened and at least a ton of it sluiced onto the slate floor. Cracks were discernible in the glittering curtain remaining in place. The rescue team shoveled coal without interruption, making certain it fell toward themselves rather than inward onto the prisoner. A voice croaked, "I'm right here, men. I can see yer light!" Within moments a hole was carved a couple of feet in diameter and a head with a lamp on it came through. Paul Dickson asked, "Are you hurt, Dad?"

"I ain't hurt, but I'm so stiff I can't move. Get me by my ankles and drag me out of here!"

When Paul grabbed his father's feet and twisted and pulled, Worley shrieked in agony, but he was freed from the trap. He was dragged through the "cat hole," placed on a stretcher, and rushed to the outside. He saw the feeble rays of the late-afternoon February sun. It was 4:30, and he had been entombed for twenty-six and a half hours. The gray hills struck him as the loveliest sight he had ever seen.

Some neighbor women covered him with blankets and gave him hot coffee. Dr. Bill Adams sent him to the Fleming hospital where he bathed, ate, and slept. He awoke at midnight and "was rarin' to go home." The doctor said he was in good shape, so he hobbled to Paul's car and they were on their way to Indian Mountain.

It came to him that he had not seen his son-in-law. "How is Ernest?" he asked, dreading the possibility that he had not escaped after all. There was a long silence. "Well, is he okay or not? Tell me the truth!" he demanded.

Paul sighed. "I hate to have to answer that question," he replied. "Ernest got out of the mine allright, and never stopped for a second trying to get you out. He worked straight for over twenty hours. Just before we got to you, he keeled over with a heart attack and was rushed to the hospital. He died a little while back when you were still asleep."

That night the second crew of tunnelers reached the remains of Dewey Rose. The flesh and bones and the blood-soaked clothing were scraped up and put in a coffin. There was nothing to embalm, and certainly nothing to view.

These miners, who shored up the weight of a mountain and tunneled under it to bring out a trapped friend, were as heroic as Alvin York and Audie Murphy were on the battlefields of two world wars. All risked their lives, and one died as a result, but so routine is death in the mines that it is little noted nor long remembered. There are no medals or citations to mark it. In the mining of coal courage is commonplace.

Ernest Bryant's family sued for payment under the work-men's compensation law. The Workmen's Compensation Board denied the claim on the grounds he had not died from traumatic injury. Judge Sam M. Ward reversed the decision, and a recovery was upheld by the Court of Appeals. The courts ruled that his death by "overwork, exposure and nervous shock" had resulted from trauma within the language of the law.

Worley Dickson was paid, too. There are some experiences from which a man never recovers, and being buried alive in a coal mine is surely one of them.

The family of Dewey Rose was paid without contest.

The litigation that grew out of the little drama inside Kona Ridge was reported in the Kentucky Decisions on January 28, 1955. (*Goebel Adams et al.* v. *Ruby Bryant et al.* 274 S.W. 2nd 791).

Two more names had joined the roster of American coal miners who have died that we might have warmth, light, and power. Some one has calculated that if all their ghostly forms were lined up head-to-toe, they would extend more than 120 miles. At the legal speed limit, a car would pass the last of them in about two hours and ten minutes.

9. Immigrants in the Mines

MOST AMERICANS who think of eastern Kentuckians envision a mix of English, Scotch-Irish, and German bloodlines that were old on this continent in 1800. In the main this perception is valid but the hills also had new immigrants from the human tidal wave that engulfed America just as the tycoons were tying the central Appalachian coal fields to the world fuel market. They came from almost everywhere to live in such places as Jenkins, Lynch, and Hellier.

Many sturdy stone houses and retaining walls in Appalachia were built by Italians who stayed on in the hills after they built the piers and abutments for the railroads. A sprinkling of Jewish and Syrian merchants came to the county seats, and the proprietor of the Coney Island Cafe in Whitesburg was Tom John, an Albanian who had hawked hot dogs for a time in New York. Perry County had a rare figure indeed, a coal operator named Allais from France.

With my father, I visited in the coal town homes of people from Sweden, Serbia, Germany, Italy, Russia, Austria, and Greece. There was even one Swiss, a wifeless mining engineer who dwelt in solitude in a spotless cottage above the town of Kona. A Croatian known as "old blind Proko" lived in a little house near my home. His eyes had been destroyed in a mine explosion and he made a meager living peddling his hand-made brooms and mops. His wife had died or returned to the old country and in his loneliness he sometimes drank too much wine and sang the saddest songs imaginable.

The janitor at the Whitesburg High School was a one-legged Russian, Steve Brosich. One morning Steve was absent and searchers found him in the furnace room hanging by a rope. He had succumbed to loneliness, poverty, and frustration, still a stranger in a strange land thirty years after he left Ellis Island.

After I was grown and practicing law in Whitesburg, the human drama sometimes brought to my office a stricken soul for whom no remedy could be found. This was true of an elderly immigrant from Serbia who called on me in 1960. He was a short, squat, broad-chested man of much strength and stamina despite his seventy years. Nonetheless, his face bore the saddest expression imaginable, with just a shade of hope that the law might be able to relieve his distress.

He had come to America on an immigrant ship just before the outbreak of the First World War. He made his way to Pittsburgh where he worked a year or two in a steel mill. When he learned that the United States Steel Company was building a huge coal-mining town on Looney Creek in Harlan County, Kentucky, he signed up to work in the mine there. He and his wife came to the new town of Lynch in time to help drive the first tunnel into the "big seam." He worked for United States Steel for nearly forty years, during which time a rejuvenated United Mine Workers of America organized the miners at Lynch and compelled "Big Steel" to finance a retirement and health care system for its employees and to pay them ever higher wages. He also experienced the far-reaching mechanization of the Lynch operations which resulted in only a few men enjoying the benefits of unionization.

His wife died during his years at Lynch and his two sons served in the Navy in World War II. When that conflict ended, they found jobs in Detroit and thereafter he seldom saw them.

In 1955 he became sixty-five and retired from the mines. He bought himself five acres up the Poor Fork of the Cumberland in Letcher County and moved his belongings to his new home. The house was a neat, old, hewed-log structure of two large rooms, probably fourteen by twenty-two feet, with extensive storage areas upstairs. He hired a man to help him and they removed the old stick and clay daubing and replaced it with cement. The outside was then weather-boarded and painted white. The old tin roof received fresh paint also, and tight-fitting new doors were installed. The ancient rose bushes were trimmed and fertilized and a thriving vegetable garden was planted and cultivated. He liked the quiet of his country retreat far from tipples, railroads, and work whistles. Insofar as the human condition will permit it, he was a happy man.

Then came calamity. During the last twenty years of his working life his wages had been generous and he had saved money regularly. He remembered with dread the failing banks and lost savings of the 1930s, so he kept his growing hoard in an old aluminum lunch pail hidden in a chifforobe. When he moved to the country, he took the pail and its contents with him. At this turn he lapsed into a form of madness.

He could not trust a bank and he feared thieves. He had guarded closely the secret of the dinner bucket and *no one* other than himself knew about his savings, which amounted to more than $30,000 in fifty and one-hundred dollar bills. He found a hiding place in the thick walls of his house. With a two-inch auger he drilled holes deep into the massive timbers. Rolls of bills were bound securely with thread, wrapped in moisture-proof coverings, and stuffed into the holes. Then he tightly fitted each hole with a peg which extended into the room about six inches. The hiding places were so spaced that the five neat pegs appeared to be perfectly natural hanging places for his hat, old coats, egg baskets, and anything else that might need to be hung up out of the way. Then, sustained by a Social Security pension and a monthly check from the United Mine Workers of America, he took his ease. He did not need much money for his simple life and in time a sixth peg took its place on the wall. With a miser's satisfaction in the money for its own sake, he was comforted by its existence but received no other benefit from it. Behind those wooden pegs lay the sweat, toil, and terrors of thousands of days at the coal face. Locked away, unknown to anyone but himself, it was safe from thieves and robbers, and from his own hands.

As his tale unfolded my dread mounted. The agonizing possibilities were almost endless. A stroke could leave him speechless and paralyzed, needing the money desperately but unable to describe its hiding place. If he were to die suddenly, his children would not receive a penny of it. In fact, it might never be found, not even by new owners of his house who could live out their days within arms' reach of a small fortune. Most frightening of all was the possibility of fire. Flames from the fireplace or stove would feed on those dry, century-old logs and would turn timbers, pegs, and money to gases and gray ash in minutes. Then the potential for good stored in those slips of green paper—a potential earned by the hardest form of industrial labor—would be irretrievably lost. I waited for the rest of the story.

As I feared, fire had come. He had heard the crackle of flames in his loft and in minutes his cherished house was a conflagration. He tried in the three or four minutes that were vouchsafed him to withdraw the pegs, but they would not yield. He succeeded only in breaking off two of them. Then the heat, and the danger that the ceiling would collapse on his head, drove him outside. All that was left were the crumpled sheets of tin from the roof and some nail-strewn ashes. As for his beloved money, no trace could be found.

He had come to inquire whether the United States treasury might restore his lost currency. He had no vestige of proof that he had ever possessed $30,000. His work with the bore holes and pegs had been solitary. To honor a claim for lost money under such circumstances would inspire similar claims after every fire, tornado, or other catastrophe. It was out of the question. He was so distraught about his loss, however, and so convinced that the "government will do right about it," that I nevertheless sent off a letter setting out his version of the facts and inquiring about the possibility of restitution. The prompt reply killed that slender hope. His face turned ashen when I read the letter to him and he left my office with slumped shoulders and shuffling gait.

I tried to encourage him about the future by pointing out that he alone knew of the money and that, by his own admission, he had no intention of spending any of it. Under these circumstances he had lost nothing but his house. He still had his two monthly checks which were an adequate living for him. I urged him to forget about his lost cash and start all over.

My urgings must have had some effect because soon afterward he returned to Lynch. Within weeks he married a widow his own age and moved into the house her husband had left her. They lived happily on the hill overlooking the ruined stump that had once been the world's largest coal tipple.

I saw him only once more, when the pair came to my office to sign a deed conveying his Letcher County land to a young couple who planned to build a new house on it. As he accepted payment for the land, he baffled his bride by asserting two or three times with much fervor, "No more pegs! No more pegs!"

About 1910, a narrow river bottom in Letcher County quite inexplicably began converting itself into a town. Contractors pushing the tracks of the Louisville and Nashville Railroad from Ravenna to McRoberts arrived with steam shovels, steam drills, and hundreds of white and black laborers. Scarcely had the twin ribbons of steel been spiked to white oak ties atop the crushed stone ballast when town builders arrived to make their fortunes in coal. A madness laid hold of otherwise sensible men and they lived and breathed coal. They were positive that the world could never get enough of it, so they built camps of cheap little houses and sought near and far for laborers to occupy them.

That little stretch of bottomland lay more or less midway between such raw new mining camps as Woodrock, Carbon Glow, and Bluefield. The owners of the land were bemused by the prospect of a perpetual boom in the valley, with spendthrift miners spreading their wages about in a high old way. Giddy with the prospect of riches, budding new capitalists found silly old capitalists who would finance their visions. Lots were surveyed and auctioned. By the new railroad line a concrete street was laid, with sidewalks to match. Carpenters and masons built residences and storehouses, a wholesale building, a railway depot, a church house or two, and a brick bank complete with a shining vault. The town was incorporated and a mayor and town council were installed.

At some point while all this was under way, a black heifer wandered onto the track and was cruelly slain by a coal drag headed down river toward the DeCoursey yards. The unfortunate beast had been much loved by the young daughter of the heifer's owner. When it came to naming the infant metropolis, this tragedy was remembered and the heifer was immortalized by the town's being given her name—Blackey. Alas, the fall of the town was as rapid as its rise and within a dozen years the glutted coal market had collapsed, the camps were emptying, the bank failed, and Blackey, Kentucky, lapsed into a slumber from which there would be no awakening.

The people who filled those three- and four-room jerry-built miners' houses came from the ends of the earth. The immigrant ships arrived daily at Ellis Island, and the Poles, Russians, Italians, and other nationalities spread across the continent in search of jobs and fortunes. Some reached Woodrock, a mile up the North Fork of the Kentucky from Blackey. Among them was a sturdy son of Imperial Russia, his staunch peasant wife, and a suckling son. He found work as a miner under a Kentucky hillside. When the boom collapsed, most immigrants left for the cities, but the Russian stayed behind. He had saved his wages and bought one of the camp houses. He raised cabbages, beets, potatoes, and corn in his garden and brewed beer for his moments of relaxation. Gradually he learned to understand English and speak it, more or less. He worked when and where wages were to be found—as a farm laborer, a section hand on the railroad, a miner when there were orders for coal, a timber cutter for logging companies, and, after the coming of the New Deal, for the W.P.A. The years slipped away and he passed from youth to old age.

In 1950 a neighbor found him dead in his little home. He was in his bed, apparently the victim of a heart attack. There was no suspicion of foul play. He had lived alone for many years and none of his neighbors remembered a wife or children. His land included an acre of rich river bottom and two acres of rocky hillside. The county attorney filed a suit alleging that he had died leaving no next of kin and asking for a judgment of escheat under which the title would revert to the Commonwealth of Kentucky. The state would then sell the property at a Master Commissioner's sale.

Judge Sam Ward of the Letcher Circuit Court, who had merited an essay in John Day's *Bloody Ground*, loved his bour-

bon whiskey. Although he had serious shortcomings as a judge,
he also had redemptive qualities. He was a Lincoln-hearted man
whose sympathies were steadfastly with workers, farmers, the
unfortunate, and the poor. Like Thomas Jefferson, he in-
stinctively mistrusted all government as tending to tyranny and
oppression. He had read the county attorney's pleadings and
asked me to come to his office. At his request I read the complaint and the escheat plea. He said, "I am appointing you
attorney ad litem to find this dead man's heirs and notify them
of his death and the filing of this suit." He smoked another of his
beloved cigarettes, then opined, "It is mighty hard for a man to
die without kinfolks. Somewhere or other this old Russian had
relatives. Do whatever it takes to find them. If there is anyway I
can prevent it, I'm not going to let the state get this old man's
property!"

The next day I obtained the key to the house from the sheriff,
to whom it had been delivered for safekeeping. The railroad
sidetrack, commissary, and tipple had long since vanished and
bushes grew on the slate dump. A few of the houses had survived
the years, the best of which I identified as belonging to the
Russian everyone in the neighborhood had known simply as
Steve. The house was a frail, four-room, weather-boarded structure that stood on stilt legs on the hillside plot. There was a front
porch with two-by-four timbers to support the roof. The original
tar-paper roof had been replaced with green-painted tin. The
structure had been painted inside and out within the last three
or four years. On a wall inside there was a calendar from a
neighborhood store and a likeness of Jesus and the disciples,
bought long ago, probably at a company commissary. The place
was clean. What little dust there was had probably collected
since the owner's death.

The furnishings were sparse: a bed and trunk, two straight
chairs, a coal-burning cook stove, a kitchen table, and an old-
fashioned kitchen cabinet. His clothing still hung inside an
improvised wardrobe. Of books and papers there were none. An
intensive search of the rooms disclosed nothing in writing.

The last item I investigated was a trunk at the foot of the bed.
It was made of metal with two clasps fitted with latches. The
locks were missing and the lid could be lifted. Inside were some

clean shirts and socks, underwear, and a neatly-folded necktie. I felt myself an interloper looking into matters not meant for my eyes.

In a corner of the trunk lay a thick, massive book bound with leather-covered wooden boards. The first page displayed a picture of Czar Nicholas II in his military cap and uniform, bordered with religious symbols. The next page portrayed Jesus bearing a cross. The words, of course, were written in the Cyrillic alphabet and were wholly incomprehensible to me. The book was obviously old, perhaps the only possession from the old country that the immigrant had preserved.

I went through the pages carefully looking for papers, and was delighted to find two letters. The envelopes had not survived, but the sheets had been wrapped in neatly creased and folded brown paper from a grocery bag. Obviously these writings were important, at least in the sentimental sense, to have justified such careful preservation within the pages of a holy book. I took the Bible and the papers to my office to look carefully for any notations that might have been written on the Bible's margins. I was going to need a translation of the papers.

Inquiries at the foreign language departments at the state's universities produced no professor who could translate the letters, so I wrote to Harvard setting out my predicament. A professor there promptly agreed to assist me and I forwarded the letters to him. Handwriting can be baffling under the best of circumstances and this specimen, the ink dim from aging, surely must have taxed the patience of the learned scholar who pored over the dimmed ink with the aid of a magnifying glass under a bright light. In his reply he pointed out that Russia is so vast, and historically so divided into cultural isolates that language often reflects local adaptations much at variance from scholarly norms.

The older letter bore a date in 1922 and was from a wife in a village near Novgorod to her husband at Woodrock, Kentucky. She and Ivan, their son, had safely returned to their home in the old country. Times were very hard in Russia. Coal and food were hard to come by, but life was much better than in Kentucky. She implored him to come back home and join them. The American coal fields were wicked places without God and with only heathen churches. No one would be blessed if he insisted on living in such a sinful place. She said that she and Ivan loved him very much.

The second letter was written in 1946. Ivan was in his thirties now and a veteran of many battles with the Germans. He had married, but his wife and child had not survived the war. He would like to see his father again but could not afford a trip to America. Besides, the government would not permit him to leave his employment or travel outside the Soviet Union. Perhaps a visit to America would be permitted sometime in the future. The letter had been read by a censor; it carried a stamped "approved" in red ink. The letters bore the same return address.

I drafted a letter to the son and sent it to the professor for translation into Russian. He sent back to me the Russian version which I signed and dispatched to the U.S.S.R. I informed Ivan of his father's death, and asked whether there were any other children and for information about his mother. I told him, also, about a surprising discovery I had made: his father had not labored all those years for nothing. In addition to his little home he had left $33,000 in a passbook account at a bank in Hazard, Kentucky. I knew that he wanted to visit his father's old home and expressed the hope that he could do so now to claim his rightful patrimony.

Weeks passed, then months. No reply came, but the letter was not returned. I wrote again. This time I received a reply, not from the heir, but from the Soviet embassy in Washington. The caller said that he was an assistant to the ambassador and was making the call at his request. It seems that Ivan had shown my letter to a Russian official with a stout avowal that he *did not* desire to go to America. He wanted the land sold and the proceeds of the sale and the money in the bank account turned over to the ambassador, who would then convert it to rubles and forward the money to Ivan. All would thus be very legal and satisfactory to everyone.

A notarized sealed document, which would be my authority, had been signed by Ivan and was being mailed to me. The embassy would send a counselor to attend the court proceedings, if necessary. I was told that Ivan's mother had died during the war and a death certificate so showing was enclosed with the other document. When I declared that Ivan should appear in court and testify under oath to all this, my caller testily replied that this was impossible. The Soviet Union was recovering from the ravages of the war and no Soviet citizen would consider leaving his work until the job had been completed.

As attorney ad litem for Ivan I reported all my acts, discoveries, and conversations to the court. The county attorney agreed that Ivan was the lawful heir and should receive the money. We acted in concert with the court to try to get him here for a hearing. Judge Ward allowed that "if we can get him over here, the Russians will never see him again. He'll take his money and head for Chicago."

But our combined efforts were of no help to Ivan. Instead we received letters from the State Department urging that the arrangement suggested by the Soviet embassy "and the heir" be approved and confirmed.

The judge, the county, and I capitulated. The master commissioner sold the house and land at auction for the sum of twelve hundred dollars. In the meantime, interest had increased the bank account to $34,000. Court costs were taxed at a few hundred dollars. Thus more than $35,000 remained for distribution to the heir, minus a fee payable to me for services in his behalf as attorney ad litem.

All was now complete except for the order fixing my fee and directing the master commissioner to pay the money by check to the Soviet ambassador, agent-in-fact for the absent Ivan. I took the order to Judge Ward with the fee omitted so he could fill it in within his reasonable discretion. The judge was smoking one of his endless cigarettes. From a bottle cached in his desk he poured himself a small dram of bourbon, sipped it, and studied the order.

After a few moments of reflection he offered an opinion. "Russia is not like this country. The government will take this man's money and convert it into rubles at *its* exchange rate. He will never get to spend a nickel of his money in this country, and the rubles won't buy anything over there. Hell, money is no good in a country that can't make toothbrushes or raise wheat! They will probably wind up sending him to Siberia just because his daddy lived in the States. Besides if it hadn't been for you, it would all have gone to the state treasurer." Then he asked, "How much do you think you ought to be paid?"

In those days $3,500 was a large sum, plenty in fact to buy a new Buick automobile. I had been hoping for that amount and planning to use it for payments on my home which was burdened by an $11,000 construction mortgage. When I mentioned that sum, he ground out his cigarette, signed the order, and wrote in some numbers. "There," he said, "go and pay off the bank in full. You need it more than Joe Stalin does."

He had fixed the fee at $11,333. To put this sum in perspective, the governor of Kentucky then was paid $10,000 annually and congressmen were yet to increase their salaries to $12,500. Ivan's inheritance enabled me to pay for my home in full and to become debt free. To say I rejoiced at the development would be an understatement.

The remainder of the money was mailed to the Soviet embassy, as the heir's designated agent, and nothing more was heard from that quarter. I wrote Ivan a full explanation of all that had happened, but my letter was returned unopened three months later. It had been stamped with some sort of seal and bore notations in Russian that I could in no wise interpret. I did not send them to the professor for translation.

Often when I enter my home, I think of my benefactors—Ivan and Judge Ward, and the unknown Russian peasant who worked so hard in an alien land, and saved so diligently, for such an unforeseen end.

I wonder, too, whether justice was done "in the premises," and just how the Goddess herself would have handled the matter had she weighed it in her scales. How would *she* have requited Ivan and me, and that strange, gigantic, menacing country Ronald Reagan would one day call "an evil empire"?

10. A Man of Honor

JAMES H. FRAZIER was born near Gate City, Virginia, in 1850 and died in Letcher County, Kentucky, ninety-five years later. Few people now remember him and soon there will be nothing to mark his hectic life except a grave marker on a knoll at Whitesburg. His life illustrates the misty nature of money, power, fame, infamy, and influence, because at one time he was the wealthiest and most influential person in his county—and later the most infamous.

The Civil War desolated western Virginia, and this may have influenced Frazier's decision to move farther west into the even narrower valleys of eastern Kentucky. It is probable that he simply followed a somewhat older Virginian, William Nichols, who had left Gate City a decade earlier. Nichols did something in Letcher County that no other resident of that bailiwick had ever taken it into his head to do. Nearly eight decades after the place was settled, most families still lived in the kind of hewed-log houses that were in vogue in frontier times. The rest lived in board-and-batten frame houses, with the few fortunate living in structures sheathed with drop-siding weatherboards. Nichols wanted something most Letcher Countians had never seen, a brick house with sturdy, thick walls, a tin roof, and paned windows. Its construction became the talk of the county, and many people came to see it rise near the courthouse on a lot facing the expanse of mud that passed for Main Street.

Nichols found clay of a proper consistency on a nearby hill and sent back to Virginia for brickmakers. Molds were made and tamped with clay, then the red rectangles of mud were packed in makeshift ovens. The resulting bricks were mortared together on a low, stone foundation. A porch with white wooden posts fronted the building, and the tin roof was painted dark green. Architecturally it was a pleasing work—simple, unpretentious, and with good lines and dimensions.

Nichols had set up a store on a neighboring lot and young Jim Frazier worked as his clerk. Jim watched the rise of the house and listened to the awed comments. The fiscal court was so impressed that when its members decided to replace the courthouse rebels had burned in 1865, the squires determined that it too should be fashioned of brick. When the plans had been approved and a contract signed for the work, it was discovered that young Frazier had bought the hill with the clay pit. He was glad, however, to sell the contractor the mud he needed and, when other people decided that they too wanted the prestige of brick homes, he was ready to supply their needs.

Jim Frazier was a handsome man in those days, with small, well-shaped features. He became bald early but his quickness of step and physical vigor did not leave him until old age reduced him at last to a slumped figure on a front porch chair, his chin resting on the crook of a walking cane. In those twilight years he sat for endless hours, perhaps reflecting on the turbulence of his long life, but his thoughts he kept to himself.

By the mid 1880s Nichols had had enough of Kentucky and returned to Virginia. For "a valuable consideration in the lawful money of the United States," Jim bought his fine house and moved into it with Cornelia, his handsome wife from Gate City. She was older than her husband, a circumstance that may have given her the fortitude to endure the outrages he perpetrated against her throughout their half-century of marriage. Jim also bought the sturdy furniture with which Nichols had furnished his home. These things had been shipped in goods wagons from Virginia and, when Jim showed off his rocking chairs, bedsteads, tables, and wash stands, many aspiring customers for similar items were born.

Jim had established lines of credit with wholesale houses in Cincinnati and Nashville, where he was known as a man who settled his accounts on time. He bought straight, well-seasoned poplar lumber and built a new store building on a corner near the courthouse. He brought in metal siding stamped to look vaguely like cut stone. This siding and the tin roof gave the new emporium an impressive appearance. It was thirty-feet wide and sixty-five-feet long, and over the front entrance was raised a neatly printed sign, ordered up from Nashville: J.H. Frazier, General Merchandise.

The store and its loading platform were swept every morning, and the windows were washed with reasonable frequency. Jim was a clean and orderly fellow and these qualities helped business. Counters ran parallel to the ceiled walls, and behind them were the long rows of shelves his wagons kept well stocked. A wagon arrived every two or three days groaning with cargoes of horse collars and hames, trace chains, horseshoes, horse blankets, currying combs, patent medicines for all real and imaginary ills, wash boards, pitchers, plates, cutlery, soap, firearms, nails, cotton overalls and shirts, brogan shoes, and "fancy clothes for ladies and gentlemen." At J.H. Frazier's a man could buy himself a blue or black serge suit, a wool hat, and splendid sharp-toed patent leather shoes. But it was the display of clothing for ladies that was most impressive. There were long-sleeved, ankle-length dresses of divers patterns and fabrics, stylish coats and jackets, ankle-hugging shoes studded with eyelets and hooks, stockings, petticoats, shawls, and "underthings." As the county began to recover somewhat from the social and economic ravages of the Civil War, aspirations rose and Jim was ready to supply the goods people so keenly desired. In eastern Kentucky, James H. Frazier was marked as an up-and-coming man.

Jim learned about land company agents who had scoured West Virginia and southwestern Virginia buying mineral tracts, and knew that they could come seeking the treasures of eastern Kentucky, also. He began buying mineral rights on a quiet and cautious scale. Most of his customers knew little or nothing about the region's geology and were quite willing to sell a long-term fortune in coal, oil, and gas for a short-term pile of merchandise. Since Jim bought at wholesale and his retail price included transportation charges, taxes, and his margin of profit he actually only paid 50 percent for the mineral deeds. Jim

might offer farmer Jones fifty cents per acre for the minerals
and comprehensive or "broadform" mining rights to his two
hundred acres. Since the one hundred dollars was paid in merchandise which had cost Jim fifty dollars, he was actually buying for twenty-five cents an acre. His stacks of mineral deeds
grew steadily, as did deeds for lots and farms near the county
seat. Time would bring railroads to the region, automobile roads
would follow, mining corporations would build twenty-seven
new coal towns in the county, and this activity would set off a
surge of growth in the county seat. Then all who would build
homes, sell automobiles, or become merchants would find that
Jim owned the lands they needed. And they would learn that he
who had bought cheaply now sold only at high prices and for
cash.

Jim did something else for which he became notorious: he
seduced his female customers. He had a monumental appetite
for the delights of the flesh and many customers yielded. Pretty
girls and handsome women were tempted by his merchandise
but lacked the dollars to buy them. Jim had the courtly manners
we associate with southern gentlemen. If a lady sighed ruefully
and looked longingly, he would ply her with propositions. Such
advances would nowadays be called sexual harassment but, be
that as it may, many accepted his advances and departed with
bundles of new clothing and small sums of money.

A great difficulty for Jim lay in the fact that he was both
potent and prepotent. This latter characteristic meant that all
the children he sired—and they were legion—looked like him.
In many parts of the county over many years, husbands congratulated themselves on the sturdy babes their wives had borne
only to perceive with indignation that, as the child grew, he
came to look exactly like Jim Frazier. The child invariably
displayed the short stature, quick energetic motions, blue eyes,
fine features, and other characteristics of the county's leading
merchant!

In the 1950s and 1960s it was not unusual to see three or four
elderly, stockily-built men and women talking animatedly to
each other on the streets of Whitesburg. Their gestures and
behavior, their laughter and good humor were identical. They
came from different communities in the county and bore a

variety of family names, but they were united by a common
bond: all were offspring of Jim Frazier and had the good sense to
laugh about it. Most of them were successful business people
and some were wealthy. A few lived quietly in Florida retirement.

Jim's procreative proclivities led to tragedy on at least two
occasions. They resulted in criminal trials that were celebrated
in the annals of Kentucky law. Each of the cases was captioned
on appeal *Frazier* v. *Commonwealth,* and confirmed a conviction
of willful murder.

One of Jim's offspring was brought into the world by a cus-
tomer of his emporium who lived on a constricted hill farm near
the headwaters of Little Cowan Creek. Her acres were on the
northwest face of the Pine Mountain, near the great jut of
sandstone known as High Rock, the loftiest elevation on the
nation's longest continuous ridge. Her son grew up in a picturesque setting but a hard one. Given the name of the man who
had fathered him in a wareroom in the back of his store, Floyd
Frazier has the grim historical distinction of being one of the
last Kentuckians to suffer death by lawful hanging.

Floyd was born in 1889 and was "strange" from the start. His
mother's husband silently and scornfully tolerated him as an
interloper, an intruder who had no lawful standing in his house.
The mother came to see him in the same light: one who by his
very being had ruined her good name, brought her a cold marital bed, and cast a pale of sorrow over her life. She regarded the
child as the hateful personification of the man who had seduced
her as a young woman, then ignored her forever after.

Treated by his family as a pariah whose every bite of food was
resented and whose presence caused a sigh or a frown, young
Floyd became a solitary soul. Unwanted by the few people he
knew, he considered others his enemies and shunned them.
When he was not at work with a grubbing hoe or plow, he roamed
the mountains alone. In the solitudes of the mighty ridge on
which he lived he lacked even the companionship of a dog. When
people passed along the rutted county road which led through
Proctor's Gap and thence to Virginia, they were studied by eyes
that were taking on the light of madness. Since few people spoke
to him, he became rusty in speech and often failed to reply to

greetings and questions. People shook their heads and said he was foolish or crazy or addled. Most of Jim Frazier's "come by chance" children were keen-witted, but this one, they said, did not have much sense.

Beyond the head of the valley on Pert Creek, on an even less promising stretch of rocky ground lived a young widow named Ellen Flannery. Her husband had died, of a fever or a runaway saw log or one of the other causes of death that stalked the hills in those days, and she was left with five children. Social Security and public assistance programs were not yet glimmers in the eyes of young Franklin Roosevelt and the youths who would one day constitute his brain trust. She had to wring food for her orphans from those bleak acres and from her chickens, cow, and pigs. A failure of those sources meant starvation.

One day in May 1907, Ellen Flannery went out to pick wild spring greens in the mountain coves. She did not return and the next morning her oldest child, a daughter of thirteen, told a passerby of her absence. Within hours several men from the community gathered to hunt for her. Among them was silent, secretive Floyd Frazier. Though they spent many hours, they found no trace of her. When darkness came, the children were taken to the home of a neighbor for the night and at daylight the hunt for the missing woman began anew.

The searchers thought it out of character that Floyd should forsake his solitude and join them. About noon as they were entering a rocky defile, Floyd pointed across the narrow valley and remarked that he would not go there for fifty dollars. "She is not there. There is no use of going there." But they went and there they found the widow Flannery. Her long brown hair had been wrapped around a bush, her throat had been slashed, and field stones had been piled on her bloating body.

The sheriff, Louis Cook, was in the party and he promptly arrested Floyd and took him to his office for questioning. Neighbors buried Ellen Flannery in a homemade coffin, and her funeral was attended by many hundreds of people whose emotions encompassed horror, grief, and vengefulness.

There was no Miranda rule of evidence in those days and Floyd was not informed of his constitutional right to remain silent. By scarcely coherent utterances he denied all knowledge of his neighbor's death. Nonetheless the suspicion that had settled on him inexorably would propel him to the gallows. And there was damning evidence; the clear, clean print of a heavy brogan shoe near the murder scene conformed perfectly to Floyd's shoe print, even to tack marks in the heel. There was also the matter of dried blood found on his shirt sleeve. He claimed it came from a nose bleed, or maybe from a chicken he had killed.

To cinch the matter a deputy sheriff swore that while he was guarding Floyd and they were alone, the prisoner admitted that he had killed her and added, "I had to do it!" This statement may have been a wholly untenable claim of self-defense, but more likely it was a reference to some morbid pathological compulsion. In any event, his admission that he had killed her would be accepted as true by two trial juries.

Jim Frazier was no stranger to courts and trials. Nearly twenty land title actions were litigated to defend or assert his claims to boundaries of coal, oil, and gas, and he always hired lawyers of proven ability. When one of his sons stood shackled and with his life at stake, Jim's ire rose. He determined that no child of his would die at the end of a rope if the guile and cunning of legal counsel could forestall it.

Jim hired not one or two but four legal luminaries, including Monroe Fields, a rapidly rising star whose legal wizardry would become legendary. But the ensuing courtroom battle was fruitless. Even Jim's special friends on the jury ignored the silent pleading in his eyes. All voted for a verdict of guilty and a sentence of death by hanging.

The desperate lawyers promptly appealed and the judgment was reversed on the astonishing, but valid, ground that the jury had received no instruction on the defendant's right of self defense. When the case was retried in 1908, the struggle intensified as all parties at the defense table faced the grim significance of a second guilty verdict. The principal hope now was pegged to a strengthened plea of innocence by reason of insanity. Physicians testified to the defendant's limited comprehension, but the jurors were unmoved. They knew Floyd Frazier was no mental wizard, but they also knew that he understood the nature of his act when he killed Ellen Flannery and knew that the act was wrong. In those days of legal common sense that was enough, and the twelve veniremen duly handed up a verdict identical to the first. On a second appeal the high court found no error.

The pathetic figure of Floyd Frazier went to the scaffold on May 19, 1910. An immense crowd gathered for the occasion, arriving on the backs of horses and mules, afoot, and in buggies and jolt wagons. The county newspaper, the *Mountain Eagle,* reported it to be the biggest crowd in the county's history.

A vicious rumor had circulated that his mother had prompted him to commit the crime, but Floyd denied the story. "My mother never gave me any bad counsel," he shouted from the scaffold. And he had some good words for "Pappy Jim." "Jim Frazier is a good man, I think; but every man has his faults. You have yours and I have mine."

A second before he died the poor distraught creature shrieked, "Good-bye to everybody forever and forever! My mother, O my mother! O Lord! O Lord!"

His mother waited at the base of the scaffold and accompanied the corpse to the burying ground. As for Jim, he stayed out of sight in his store until the ringing of the schoolhouse bell announced the physician's report that the felon's pulse had ceased.

The newspaper reported that the vast "concourse" of people then spent an unprecedented sum of money in the town's stores, but Mr. Frazier sold a mere twenty-five dollars' worth of merchandise. "Because of the sadness of the day he made no special effort for business."

But all too soon Jim was back to business as usual in all respects. Like King Solomon he loved many strange women, and the strangest of them all was Ulsey Banks. Ulsey was the wife of William Banks, a quiet, patient farmer who lived a dozen miles from Jim's store. We know that he was a patient and enduring man because of the commendably calm manner in which he suffered the outlandish behavior of Jim and Ulsey.

We do not know how Jim first discovered Ulsey's delights, but he did discover them and found her irresistible. She began coming to town much more frequently than was to be expected of a farmer's wife and, more often than not, she returned with new clothing, money, and various desirable household items.

Will Banks investigated and learned that on each of these trips his wife spent inordinate lengths of time on the premises of James H. Frazier, General Merchandise. Then he was told by his daughter that she had discovered Jim and her mother in intimate privacy in a darkened room at Will's own house. Some time later, returning home from a Masonic Lodge meeting, he found the passionate pair in bed together. Outraged beyond the limits of patience, he shot Jim, but unfortunately for him the pistol was of small calibre and the bullet only inflicted a relatively minor flesh wound in the merchant's arm.

After that Will decided to rid himself of his untrustworthy wife and to garner a bit of money for his own purse. He sued her for divorce and sued Jim for damages, alleging that he had alienated her affections for her husband, seduced her, and destroyed the domestic quietude of his household. All these revelations and developments left Jim short of temper and lusting for vengeance.

On the morning of November 9, 1917, Jim glanced out the door of his store and saw Will Banks in front of the courthouse. He was leaning against a concrete post, staring with hatred in his eyes in the direction of the sanctuary of the man who had cuckolded him. When Will turned away to walk across the street, Jim seized a Marlin high-powered rifle, thrust a cartridge into it, aimed it precisely, and fired. The bullet struck Banks in the back, killing him instantly.

It was a raw damp day and people were indoors. Jim had stood well back from the open door so the building absorbed most of the gun's report. Behind a counter at floor level there was a loose ceiling board which Jim pulled out a few inches. He shoved the rifle into the open space between the timber studs, restored the board and shoved a box of woolen blankets against it.

The dead man was noticed by someone in the courthouse and Monroe Fields, the commonwealth attorney, was notified. Fields surmised that the heavy bullet had felled its victim so instantaneously that the alignment of his body was unchanged. Within minutes he found the bullet, deep embedded in the facing of a heavy wooden door. The eraser end of a pencil was inserted into the hole and the sharpened end pointed directly to the door of J.H. Frazier, General Merchandise. When Fields and the sheriff arrived, Jim was sweeping the floor, much concerned with the neatness of the premises. He expressed surprise when told the cause of their visit.

A preliminary search of the place revealed no firearm except some new ones in merchandise racks and clogged with grease. Certain he was right, Fields ordered that all the merchandise be taken from the shelves and the walls be made bare. He then meticulously inspected the walls. All the ceiling boards were of tough yellow poplar, securely nailed and painted over. Fields examined the baseboards. Where the box of blankets had sat there was a board like all the others, the outlines of nail heads visible under the paint, but the nails were not driven into timbers. When Fields tugged at the loose board, it moved outward, revealing a cash box and the walnut stock of a .41-calibre Marlin rifle, its muzzle smelling of fresh gunsmoke.

Jim's life turned hellish. He was promptly indicted for murdering a peaceful man whose wife he had seduced and whose home he had lecherously invaded. Jim's sexual excesses generally had been regarded with humor and no little envy, but now he was denounced as an adulterer, venal and corrupt beyond words. He had shot in the back an unarmed man who had relied on the law for justice—a commendable course not often followed in the violent hills. Complicating his predicament beyond measure was the fact that Banks was a Mason in a county in which the brotherhood was strong. Monroe Fields set out to obtain for Jim the same fate that had been imposed upon his bastard son.

Because he was wealthy and influential, Jim was usually surrounded by numerous toadies and hangers-on, but he now found himself forsaken and alone. Late at night as he pondered the consequences of his impetuous crime, he realized that his hold on life was extremely tenuous. A man with vast holdings of timber and land and the capacity to marshal impressive sums of money, he faced the possibility that he would be among the first to die in Kentucky's new electric chair.

Jim's case was exceedingly weak and he tried to bolster it by hiring a battery of skilled lawyers. Gathered from Booneville, Prestonsburg, Whitesburg, Winchester, and Lexington, they were retained as much for their influence with the people of the county as for their legal skills. The five barristers included Dan

Fields who, as commonwealth attorney, had prosecuted Floyd.
Monroe Fields, who had defended Floyd, was now the commonwealth attorney who would prosecute Jim.

When court convened, the judge ordered that a panel of jurors
be summoned from Clark County, thus depriving Jim of the
slender hope that a "special friend" might hang the jury and tire
the prosecution. The jurors were not hesitant; they found Jim
guilty of murder. The skill of Winchester lawyer J.M. Benton
may have persuaded them to fix his punishment at life imprisonment rather than death by electrocution.

Jim could breathe a deep sigh of relief. He was locked up in
the Letcher County jail pending an appeal, but his crafty mind
realized that the door could be swung open.

The jailer gave his distinguished prisoner a special room
where he could enjoy privacy and avoid the uncouth villains who
occupied the cells. A bedstead brought from his home was fitted
out with a feather bed, pillows, and a bolster. A huge oak rocking
chair was placed by the bed and a small walnut writing table
(which is now in my living room) provided comfortable and
convenient workspace.

He sent for his land lawyer, David Hays, and set him to work.
From the law office and from the jail cell went forth letters to
land corporations and to their officials and lawyers. In due time
replies were received. Deeds were drafted, signed and mailed.
Jim was selling his mineral lands on a large scale, shamelessly
driving hard bargains, even though in prison. Crisp blue checks
drawn on Philadelphia, Pittsburgh, Boston, and New York
banks passed between the bars of his cell and were endorsed and
returned to Hays. They found lodgment in distant banks under
the attorney's name as agent for his client. Shortly before the
court of appeals confirmed the circuit judgment, Hays entrained
for Frankfort.

Wilson Fields, whose father was Jim's attorney on the appeal,
knew most things of importance that happened in the county.
When he told me the story of the Fraziers and their downfall, he
told me he was certain that Hays's briefcase contained $100,000
in five, ten, and twenty dollar bills. In impoverished Kentucky
that was a lot of money in 1918. Despite the inflation set off by
World War I it had immense purchasing power. It was a time

when a United States senator drew $8,000 annually and the governor of Kentucky was paid $6,000. A man with $100,000 could retire and live comfortably on the interest it would pay.

On December 20, 1918, the Kentucky Court of Appeals handed down an opinion that carefully detailed the evidence and disclosed no scintilla of support for a new trial. Both the law and the evidence supported the verdict.

A few days later the prisoner was led by the sheriff and jailer before the circuit judge, who asked whether either the defendant or his lawyer could show any ground or reason why the verdict of the jury and the judgment of the court should not be made final. Hays rose, drew a paper from his briefcase, and handed it to the judge. His Honor read it with obvious perplexity and amazement. He gestured to the commonwealth attorney. When the youthful prosecutor read the document bearing the great seal of the Commonwealth at its head and a bit of blue ribbon near its end, all color drained out of his face and he sagged into a chair. Governor Augustus O. Stanley had granted the defendant a full and complete pardon.

To say that the governor's action stirred a storm of outrage would be an understatement. There were mutterings about a lynch mob, but nothing came of it. The bed, chair, and table went back to the house and Jim returned to his store. A few years later, after Jim's long-suffering wife Cornelia was gathered to her eternal home, Jim united with Ulsey Banks in what the preacher chose to call the bonds of holy matrimony.

In 1919, Augustus Stanley was the Democratic candidate for the United States Senate. Speaking at the Letcher County courthouse in the fiery oratory of the day, he exhorted people to rally around his banner to continue the march of progress the development of the coal fields had set off in the Kentucky mountains. He searched the crowd but could not see the face of the man his executive pardon had saved from a life of hard labor in the state penitentiary. "Where," he inquired, "is Jim Frazier?"

Jim was at home enjoying a glass of Virginia Gentleman in his jailhouse rocking chair. Annoyed, the governor observed to a local Democratic wheelhorse that he wanted to visit Jim after the speaking.

My friend Wilson overheard the remark and, as the meeting

broke up, hastened across the street to inform Jim of the approach of the grand man and his entourage of local Democrats. Both Wilson and Jim were rock-hard Republicans and for the rest of his days Wilson loved to tell what happened on that fall afternoon.

A low fire burned on the grate, driving off some of the autumn chill. Jim sat nursing his glass when the rap at the door announced the arrival of the distinguished visitor. Jim bade them "Come in." When his excellency entered, Jim sat stolidly staring at him. He neither rose nor greeted the ex-governor. Stanley was clearly baffled. He looked about him, shook hands twice with Wilson, then extended his hand to Jim, whose grip was notorious for its firmness. Jim extended a hand that was as limp as a dead fish. The governor grasped it, then let it go.

"Mr. Frazier," he began, "I am much disappointed that you did not come to my speaking though it was within fifty yards of your front door. And now that I have come hat in hand to visit you in your home, you show me inhospitality and discourtesy. I find this impossible to understand in view of the fact that it was my executive pardon that set you free to enjoy your home and friends." Then after a pause, "I had hoped that you would be active in support of my campaign."

Wilson said that Jim looked the hapless candidate up and down, and scorn was in his eye. "I owe you no support, or appreciation, or anything else. You got the money and I got the pardon, and that left us even." Then after another tiny sip from the glass, "I, sir, am a man of honor, and a man of honor will not support a crook." He swung the rocker around so that he was facing the fiery grate. "Good day, gentlemen," he declared, "and please close the door as you go out."

My father said that in a conversation long after the event, David Hays confirmed this account of the governor's visit, but declined to comment on the validity of Jim's claim that the governor had been paid for the pardon. Whatever the truth of the matter, Stanley was elected to the Senate but J.H. Frazier was not among those who voted for him. His integrity prevented that.

Jim lived until 1945. Twenty of those years were spent with Ulsey, who in marriage proved herself a harridan and a torment.

Her rages resounded across the growing town so that Jim found little peace at home or at the store. As for the latter, it withered to a collection of unsold and unsalable antiques until the place was cleared by a general sale in 1940. Jim lived on coal royalties and an occasional sale of land until age rendered him helpless in body and mind.

At his funeral there were numerous middle-aged men and women who resembled the Jim of earlier decades. The gravestone beside his own clearly commemorates his first wife. His fiery second wife is buried elsewhere in an unremembered spot, their passion dead long before they were. All his getting and losing, his hates and fervors and turbulence are also dead and gone, as are his sons and his daughters. And therein lies a moral, if one can discover it.

11. Old Carl Brought Him Out

JIM PERKINS OF KNOTT COUNTY was famous for his immense hands and his enormous mustache that extended across his wide upper lip to vast mutton-chop sideburns. He would seize a voter with those ham-sized paws and draw him close to whisper in his ear. When Jim whispered a confidence, his whiskers tickled the voter's cheek and ear. Practically everyone in the county had been so treated and, in consequence, they elected and reelected Perkins to the office of county attorney.

Jim's son, Carl D., had his father's giant hands and hulking form. He would seize a voter in his bear-like embrace, conduct him to one side for a whispered chat, and win him over to the proposition that Carl should be in Congress. By a huge majority the people in his east Kentucky district kept Carl in Congress for thirty-five years. Then they swept his son, Carl C., into the office to begin the cycle anew. The young congressman possesses the same physical characteristics so conspicuous in his father and grandfather.

I first met Carl D. Perkins during the administration of Governor Earle Clements. I went with my father and Doc Wright, the county political strong man, and two or three others, to "see the governor about a road." He perceived that the requested rural highway project was of vital importance to the public welfare and agreed that "Doc" Beauchamp, the rural highway commissioner, should get it underway forthwith. As one good turn deserves another, he made a request of us. It appeared to him that Judge Eddy Hill of Prestonsburg, Dr. John

Hall of Johnson County, and "Saw-loggin' Doug" Hays, all announced candidates, were exceedingly fine men and superb
Democrats, but the governor detected some shortcomings in
each. Hill and Hall were somewhat "unpredictable," he allowed,
while Doug was too old. Now, there was another fellow the
governor was trying to persuade to run—a young lawyer in the
Department of Highways who had all the necessary sterling
qualities: he was a fine Democrat, and was dependable, loyal,
and competent. But he was hesitant about taking the plunge. If
we would drop by this fellow's office in the Highway Department
and urge him to make the race, the governor would be grateful.

Dr. Wright inquired about the man's identity and we were
told "He is Carl Perkins from Knott County." "Who in the hell is
Carl Perkins?" the puzzled county chairman demanded in be-
wilderment.

A few minutes later we were at the office of Attorney Perkins.
We found Carl composing a legal brief. After the introductions
had been made and chairs found, Doc made a surprising revela-
tion. Drawing his chair close to Carl's desk and looking him in
the eye he declared, "Carl, we have come by to ask you to run for
Congress. There is a big ground swell for you in Letcher County."

This unexpected but flattering news caused Carl to blush
with pleasure, but he demurred because of the cost of a campaign. He was, he said, a veteran and needed to catch up on
earnings lost during the war. Doc explained that he could catch
up in Congress. "You needn't be out any money. You can continue to draw your salary, and arrangements can be made to let
you drive a state car that has no decals on it. Your friends will
raise the money you need. Come on and run! Nineteen forty-
eight is your year!"

A couple of weeks later Carl announced that he was entering
the race for Congress. He said that many of the political leaders
had urged him to run and that he wanted to serve the people of
the district. His sympathies were with the little folks and he was
a "New Dealer who hoped to continue the policies of Franklin
Delano Roosevelt."

Carl was nursing a sore arm at the time. He had been helping
a neighbor put new shoes on a mule when the willful animal

showed his disapproval by delivering a vicious kick. Carl was
always the kind of man who would help someone and that is why
he went to Congress while Harry Truman was president and
stayed there, accumulating seniority and influence, while Presi-
dents Truman, Eisenhower, Kennedy, Johnson, Nixon, Ford and
Carter came and went.

Carl *was* a New Dealer whose service came long after FDR
announced the demise of "Dr. New Deal." He embraced the spirit
of Harry Truman's Fair Deal, then the notions of John Kennedy's
New Frontier. He embraced with a whole heart Lyndon
Johnson's Great Society. Carl was a "good old boy" who wanted to
do things for the good old boys back home, and for the good old
girls, too. Carl was an unwavering believer in the notion that
federal funds should flow without stint into the Seventh Kentucky District. The upstanding people of the district overwhelmingly endorsed his doctrines and practices and he never faced a
serious challenge. All his opponents in seventeen consecutive
elections were buried under landslides. Finally his adversaries
gave up and quit running against him. They wearied of beating
their heads against the solid phalanxes of voters who lined up
behind "Carl D."

Carl was an unabashed enthusiast for what Franklin Roosevelt was the last president to call the dole. He voted for a vast
array of good things. His "aye" rang out in good times and bad,
in booms and busts, during many deficits and a few surpluses.
His labors were linked to the Accelerated Public Works Program
that financed new courthouses for pauper counties. He was
behind appropriations to provide Aid for Dependent Children,
the Kerr-Mills medical assistance measure, then Medicaid and
Medicare. He was for WIC—good food for Women, Infants and
Children. There were measures to provide pensions for miners
with black lung, to extend social security benefits to the sick and
disabled, and to build houses for the poor and fix up existing
shacks. Mixed in with these came federal aid to education, and
federal agencies poured out unprecedented torrents of money to
improve the public schools. (Alas, they got worse by the year.)
Then came the Appalachian Development Commission with
federal funds to build improved highways, finance nursing
homes and hospitals, establish vocational schools, and do count-

less other desirable things. The list is almost endless. By the end of Carl's days in Congress capitalistic America was paying more money to assist its dependent people than all the rest of the world combined. Predictably, the number of the "disadvantaged" expanded faster than appropriations could be made for them.

Carl did not rest with the passage of legislation. If a needy old boy was denied his social security benefits, a letter to Carl would result in a call to the Social Security administrator. If necessary, he would call the White House. Carl once called Lyndon Johnson from a Christmas Eve dinner to acquaint him with the desperate need of Breathitt County for a new courthouse. I have seen disallowed claims reversed in short order after Carl was made familiar with the facts.

All these activities in Washington produced not only the programs to aid the doleful but bureaucracies to administer the programs. The bureaucrats were as grateful to Carl as were those who received the benefits. The unbeatable congressman became ever more unbeatable. For all practical purposes everybody was for Carl. The dissidents were so few as to be no threat to him. Only the march of time could undo him.

Carl D., as he was universally called, was easily the most beloved Kentucky Congressman of this century and perhaps in the state's history. He simply had no enemies. If someone persisted in opposing him, Carl would feel a deep hurt about it, but animosity was not in him. He was always ready to forget the past and do an opponent a favor. The people were united in their approval. Not even Henry Clay in his Bluegrass stronghold had marshalled such favor and affection.

For one thing, Carl did not want to be governor of the state or a United States senator. He was perfectly content to be a congressman from the Seventh District. He came to know the people in that vast sprawl of twisting ridges as intimately as most people know their brothers and sisters. Carl was not a Mr. or Mrs. man. With him it was John and Sallie and Mabel and Bill. In return, nobody ever called him congressman or Mister Perkins. The humblest ragamuffin called him Carl D.

He had a prodigious memory for names and faces. He was aided in this respect by his habit of writing a memorandum about a new acquaintance. Even while he was talking to a person, the little notebook would come out and the immense hand would jot down name, place, description, and other information. After that there was total recall and a first-name relationship.

A letter to Carl never went unanswered. The reply was prompt and helpful. And people wrote to him on everything from IBM Selectrics and word processors to pencilled scrawls on pulp paper. How he kept up with the monumental flow of paper is one of the mysteries of Kentucky history.

Carl was a human traffic jam. Once upon a time I saw his mud-spattered Chevrolet stop in Salyersville and the traffic immediately slowed, then came to a standstill, as people yelled to him, then jumped out to shake his hand.

One morning the huge grinning face appeared at my office in the Daniel Boone Hotel building at Whitesburg. Carl had just "dropped by and could only stay a minute." But he was not destined to get away so easily. Within moments the word was out that Carl D. was there and people jammed my waiting room. I wound up turning over a conference room to him and he held court for four and a half hours. Everyone who talked to him urged him to come for a visit, and received a promise of help.

His personal honesty was legendary. Once he parked his grimy car near my office but had no coins for the parking meter. I inserted them for him and forgot the matter. A few days later I received a cordial note thanking me for my kindness. Two dimes were attached with scotch tape to the bottom of the sheet.

He long ago stopped accepting campaign contributions. He did not need them. About 1975 he was at my office for some reason and I reached for my checkbook. The big hand motioned me to put it back in the drawer. "If I need some help, I will let you know," he said. And truly he needed no campaign funds except to pay for gasoline for his muddy car and a few similar items. Everybody was for him anyway.

He did not allow the perpetual rise of new voters to create a population of strangers. In his long tenure an entire population died or became incapacitated by age. Carl kept up with the new people, meeting them at high schools, on college campuses, and in homes. When Carl stopped at a house to see the parents, he hunted up the children, too. He got their names, talked to them about school or jobs, and enlisted them in his army of supporters. At eighteen they went to the polls for Carl D.

I encouraged a student at the University of Kentucky to write a paper about him. The lad was from Louisville and was hesitant about contacting the congressman. He called his Washington office and Carl was on the phone in moments, all cordiality and helpfulness. Carl was going to be at his Hindman home that weekend. He told the student how to find his house and when to be there. The young man met Carl at the appointed time and experienced an unforgettable weekend.

Carl greeted him kindly and warmly. The closed house was opened so fresh air could sweep away mustiness. The chairman of the House Committee on Health, Education and Welfare took food out of a deep freezer and cooked his guest a big "old timey country supper," then washed up the dishes. He explained that they had a lot of work to do tomorrow and put his guest to bed at the unheard of hour of eight o'clock.

The chairman had his guest out of bed by five the next morning. He fed him a mammoth breakfast of hot biscuits, sausage, and eggs. By six o'clock they were on the road. The first house they stopped at was steeped in darkness. The congressman and the student climbed the steps to the front porch and the huge hand pounded on the locked door. From within came an angry, "Who is it?" Carl called, "It's me, Carl Perkins." The tone changed. "Just a minute Carl. Let me get my britches on."

The daughter of the household had been in Washington with her graduating highschool class. They had been photographed in front of the Capitol with Carl. He had brought them an enlarged copy of the photograph suitable for framing. Carl pointed her out as the prettiest girl in the bunch. The sleepy young woman arrived at this point and Carl greeted her by her first name and called her "honey." The entire household beamed.

The good woman absolutely insisted on cooking breakfast. The student was stuffed and so was Carl, but they sat down and ate again. When they were driving away, Carl gave his new friend a political maxim: "Never turn down a woman's cooking. If she cooks it, you eat it and brag on it!"

All day long they visited people, great numbers of people. There were state senators, coal miners, coal operators, welfare recipients, bankers, county judges, a state representative, sheriffs, school teachers, students, and old men and women hobbling on canes. Wherever they went it was the same. Everyone was eager to see the congressman and the congressman was delighted to see them.

The student reported that they ate at least six meals and swilled a dozen or more Coca-Colas set up for them by country grocers and well-wishers. The student met a swirl of people under an indescribable diversity of circumstances. Carl put his new friend to bed early, then packed him off on Sunday morning because the congressman had to drive back to Washington. Carl took a fruitcake out of the deep freeze and cut it in two. He wrapped half of it tightly in aluminum foil and told the student to take it to his mother. "My wife, Verna Mae, made it by her special recipe. Tell your mother Carl and Verna sent it to her."

When the student reported on his adventures, he could scarcely articulate his feelings about the congressman, but of one thing he was entirely certain: "Carl Perkins will never be beaten at the polls. He will die in office. A good man or woman with a $10 million campaign chest couldn't defeat him."

In 1984, while still a congressman, Carl died of a heart attack suffered on an airplane coming into the Lexington airport. His district mourned his death with a grief that was genuine and deep. If the Seventh District had been peopled with Catholics instead of Baptists and Methodists, a petition for canonization would long since have reached the Vatican.

I felt a sincere and very real loss. I was genuinely fond of the big, hulking man with the giant hand, iron grasp, and quick grin. However history may judge his work, he was a just man with the best of intentions. His tenure in Congress is probably the longest in the state's history.

I had an experience in 1974 that tells more about him than any of the flowery eulogies read at his funeral. A smallish coal operator came to consult me about some legal matter I have long since forgotten. He was prospering in a modest way and was certainly not poor. He was one of the myriad of Americans who started life with many disadvantages and surmounted them with prolonged hard work (and with more good fortune than they are willing to admit).

In the course of our discussion we talked about the impending race for Congress, and he delivered himself of some harsh opinions about the works of Carl Perkins. Carl's support for welfare programs was leading the nation to insolvency and collapse. The moral fiber of the mountain people was being sapped by public assistance policies that picked them up before they were born and carried them until they were dead and buried. The young were learning dependency from their parents and were reaching adulthood as confirmed loafers and "no accounts." Working people were being encouraged to waste their wages rather than save them because they could rely on the government to look after them in old age. The counties and cities were coming to count on Washington instead of relying on their own resources and initiative. He ended up with, "The country is going to hell and Carl Perkins has done more to cause it than anybody in the Congress."

Then he sat for several minutes sadly and silently looking at his hands which decades of work in coal mines had made thick and calloused. He sighed. "I have talked to Carl about it, and pleaded with him with all my heart to change his thinking—but he just grins at me and pats me on the back."

It was the first of the month and he looked out the window at carloads of rural people heading for the Bank of Whitesburg to cash their welfare checks. When he looked back at me there was real anguish in his eyes. "Yes, Carl is helping to wreck the country and I know it, but I will vote for him against any man or woman on this earth! I have to vote for him no matter what he does." To say that this astounded me would be a mighty understatement. Naturally, I asked him why he had to vote for a man whose public life he regarded as destructive to the nation. His answer left no room for disagreement.

A long time before when he was a skinny young man of twenty in the uniform of a United States infantryman, he was in the battle of Huertgen Forest, which he believed was the most ferocious battle of World War II. Carl Perkins, several years older, was buck sergeant in another platoon. The Germans fought grimly and viciously from pillboxes and huge concrete bunkers. Sometimes the small arms fire was so intense that even large pine trees were cut down. My visitor's squad advanced up a smoke-filled hollow to try to pitch a satchel charge of explosives onto a pillbox that had already crumpled an entire platoon. They were seen by the Germans, who cut them down with rifles and machine guns. He was seriously wounded and those of his comrades who were not killed beat a hasty retreat, the satchel charge unused.

He lost much blood. The shadows of evening filled the hollow and its shattered trees. Dust and smoke boiled through the air. He knew good and well that he would die in a little while if he received no help because he was wholly unable to help himself. Bullets from both sides showered him with bark and needles from the shadowing branches. "I knew I was a goner," he said.

Some impulse caused him to look down the ravine and his heart stirred with hope. A United States soldier was following the water course with a long country stride. He carried no rifle or pack but had picked up a tree branch which he was using as a walking stick. He was a big man with broad shoulders and a roundish Celtic head. He reached the wounded lad in a running crouch.

"Now, don't you worry. I'll get you out of here and back to a medic in a few minutes. If it hurts when I pick you up, just chew on the tip of your field jacket collar. You can stand it!"

He swung the boyish soldier to his shoulders and held him there with one hand while the other grasped the stick. He did not put his burden down a single time until they reached a captured bunker a mile away. A field medic who was working in its shelter administered first aid and morphine. Then litter bearers carried him to a jeep and he was borne to a field hospital. "I draw for twenty percent disability," he said.

There was something else. He was sure the Germans saw his rescue. "When he picked me up, they could have machine-gunned us or killed us with mortars. But they didn't do it and I will never know why."

I waited for the rest of the story. "It was Carl. Old Carl brought me out. He just volunteered and did it. He didn't have to come for me, but he did anyway. What the hell! If he wrecks the whole damn country, I will be for him to the end."

I had found one of the few mountaineers who not only opposed Carl's political policies but deeply and keenly abhorred them. But his strong political disagreement was no match for his affection for the man. Death, which missed them both that day in Huertgen Forest, has overtaken them in the years since I heard that tale. And I suspect it also long ago claimed the German machine gunners who for unknowable reasons held their fire for a few vital moments.

12. Lawyers for the People

A FEW YEARS AGO the National Commission on Education reported, in *A Nation at Risk,* a chronicle of the sorry state of American schools, "If an unfriendly foreign power had attempted to impose on America the mediocre educational performance that exists today, we might well have viewed it as an act of war." I wholeheartedly agree.

The decline seems to have begun soon after World War II. It has continued apace amid ever-growing outlays for buildings, libraries, cafeterias, school buses, counselors in every imaginable field, ministrations of psychologists, the hubbub of countless public hearings, and a plethora of college degrees among all who teach, plan, and administer.

By contrast, the greatest person Kentucky can claim as a native son had less than a year of instruction, and that in what he called "A,B,C schools." Those schools were conducted in floorless log cabins with smoke holes instead of chimneys and no lunchrooms, libraries, or counselors. Yet Lincoln has been immortalized in bronze on the campus of Oxford University as one whose mastery of the English language "has been seldom equalled and never surpassed."

In its backwoods era America reaped a remarkable harvest of eloquence, literateness, and mathematical and scientific competence from preposterously poor schools. Why, then, do its comparatively splendid facilities and faculties now graduate such unknowing multitudes who can do nothing well? A century ago America was by current definition a backward, poor, and undeveloped country, and the Appalachian hinterland was the most disadvantaged of all. In my law office I heard of many Lincolnesque ascents from dirt-floor cabins to education, influence, and wealth, and none can be accounted for by any currently popular explanation. A mountain expression often applied to this phenomenon holds that "it just happened." I have a feeling that motivation for education and advancement is not yet understood; that where it exists, it will overcome practically any difficulties; and that where it is lacking, no remediation or guidance counseling can instill it.

In 1800 a young hunter named Isaac Newton Fields came into eastern Kentucky on a long hunt. His grandson, LeRoy Wilson Fields, stated that Isaac was born in 1776 and so was twenty-four at the time of this solitary sojourn in the wilderness. He climbed the ridges and followed the game trails and traces in what became in 1842 Letcher County. Why he chose that wild, unbroken, rough, tree-grown wilderness as a home can only be guessed. What is now the county contained at that time no more than two or three houses—tiny round-pole affairs put up to shelter families while traps were set for beavers and black bears, and an acre or two of ground was cleared for corn. In any event, he liked the country, and two years later he left his father's home in Culpepper County, Virginia, never to return. He brought with him the simple tools of a land surveyor and two or three books. He took up his abode on King's Creek (so called because a man of that name had previously carved his name on a beech tree at its mouth), surveyed a territory for himself, and made himself at home.

We can surmise a few things about Isaac Newton Fields. Apparently his parents were people of some education and they knew about and admired the great English scientist who gave the world the theory of gravity. (In the years since the first Isaac arrived, innumerable people have named their sons for him so that the land abounds in men and boys known variously as Isaac, Ice, Ike, Newton, and Newt.) We also can assume that his parents wanted him to be educated, because he had mastered the "mystery" of surveying and brought with him a small collection of books. As people moved in from Virginia and the Carolinas, he made a living measuring their lands and acting as a land agent, filing surveys, and petitioning for patents. These newcomers begot sons and daughters, so he built a log school-house and sent out a notice that he would conduct three-month subscription terms. For a dollar per month he would teach the child the alphabet, to read the Lord's Prayer and the first chapter of Genesis, and to cipher to "the rule of three." Students who returned for subsequent terms studied elements of land survey-ing, took up somewhat more lofty labors in arithmetic, read some poems and scriptural passages and declaimed them, and learned to write legibly. A student who attended this school probably walked an average of more than five miles each way, brought with him such food as he ate, and was lucky if he had any kind of book to study. If he attended three such terms, he was exposed to almost exactly the same formal education that en-abled Lincoln to compose the Gettysburg Address and the Emancipation Proclamation.

For some unknown reason this promising backwoods ped-agogue took no wife in his early years of virile manhood. But it appears from traditions passed on by his descendants that in 1823 he found a fresh mountain maiden named Alcy Day and married her when he was forty-seven and she was thirteen. Alcy is reputed to have been a niece of "Indian Fighting" John Day, the Simon Kenton of Tennessee. Their first child, Sally, was born the next year and was still alive in 1921 at age ninety-seven. At that advanced age she rode a horse wherever and whenever she wanted, and mounted unaided. Alcy bore thirteen other chil-dren over a reproductive span that totalled thirty years and gave birth to their last child on August 3, 1853. They were a hardy pair. He died at age eighty-eight in 1864, and she went the way of all flesh at ninety-four.

Their youngest son was named for the intrepid prophet who was undaunted by the lion pit of Nebuchadnezzar. As the older children grew up and married, Isaac and Alcy gave them farms. They received such strips of bottomland as the narrow valley of King's Creek affords. By Daniel's turn there was little to inherit and he received what was left—a tiny strip of flat land and a couple of hundred acres of steep, yellow-clay hillside at the head of the creek. Perhaps he did better in life than his brethren because, like the biblical Joseph, he was a deprived child.

All save one of the fourteen married and stayed close to the homeplace. LeRoy Wilson moved to Missouri where he prospered, becoming successively a county judge and a state senator. Daniel named his son for this departed brother, and my long-time friend, LeRoy Wilson Fields, believed the name was that of Isaac's father.

Something stirred in young Dan Fields. He was not content with a living wrung from hardscrabble acres at the head of a gloomy creek valley. From his father he learned to read, to write legibly and well, and to add, multiply, divide, and subtract. His father died before the boy was eleven, in the midst of Kentucky's greatest cataclysm.

By the beginning of the Civil War in 1861 the nineteen-year-old county at the extreme headwaters of three major Kentucky streams was making slow but commendable progress. A frame courthouse had been raised on a strip of bottomland the legislature had optimistically declared a town and called Whitesburg. A little road work was accomplished each year. Isaac Fields led a life-long campaign for general compulsory education and, though he did not live to see his plans written into law, he did see the beginning of publicly-financed schools. In 1857 there were 1,069 school-age children in the county's twenty-seven districts. The school term was three months and average daily attendance was 309. The county spent $1,282.80 to support its common schools.

The war brought an abrupt and bloody halt to this progress. The county's proximity to Virginia aroused nearly a thousand young men to organize a regiment that became the thirteenth Kentucky Confederate Cavalry. Others joined the Union Army or entered the Home Guard. Before long a federal army from Ohio drove the Confederates out of the Big Sandy valley. A minor battle routed the rebels at Pound Gap. The county became a seething arena of raids, counterraids, ambushes, and retaliations. Families and what sociologists now call extended families fell out, divided, and went to war within themselves and against one another. When the war ended, the county was desolate. The new courthouse and all the hewed-log school buildings were in ashes. All public offices were vacant—no one dared assume official duties and responsibilities in the midst of such rampant violence. By special act the legislature authorized Letcher Countians to probate wills in Harlan. The war ravaged Letcher more severely and more deeply than any other of the state's counties.

The first half-dozen years after Appomattox were so impoverished and filled with turmoil that there was little reconstruction, but Dan managed to find and read enough books that he was able to obtain a teaching certificate in 1871. Two years later he moved to the county seat where he could continue to earn about twenty-five dollars a month as a teacher and where he read law in the circumscribed libraries of the local barristers. In those days would-be attorneys were examined by a committee of lawyers and admitted to the bar by order of a circuit judge. Under this system he became an attorney-at-law when he was thirty. There was little to litigate in the hills in the 1880s so he ran for sheriff and was elected in 1888. Dan was a sturdy, raw-boned man with a strong will and a quick wit. He was remembered as bull-headed and quick-tempered. He was a fine lawyer.

Dan Fields courted and won tall, handsome Ritter Musselwhite, the daughter of Joe Musselwhite, a Choctaw Indian who lived on Line Fork Creek. Joe had begun life in the Jackson Purchase among the Chickasaws. He was an infant when that territory was bought for Kentucky and most of the Indians moved to Alabama. Later they were removed forcibly to Oklahoma. Musselwhite's parents did not follow the tribe. They and others made their way from the flatlands of the Purchase across the Pennyroyal and the Knobs, and hid out in the hills. When Joe grew up, he farmed, bred horses and cattle, and was in all outward respects "a civilized Indian," as people would have said at that time. He married a white woman and she bore him two daughters, Ritter and Rachel.

Squire Jesse Day remembered Joe Musselwhite in his old age. He said that the one-time fugitive from the removers was tall and very slender. He wore a black hat with a hard, flat, straight brim. His hair was combed back into a single ropelike braid which fell to his shoulders and was bound with a silver clasp. He carried a keen knife in a scabbard at his side and walked with a long, easy gait, his hands clasped together behind his back. "Joe Musselwhite was not a man to tamper with," he said.

In his middle years Musselwhite lived at Little Cowan Creek closer to Whitesburg, and the hewed-log house he built still stands. Passers-by who notice it at all see only a weather-beaten storage shed for hay and tools.

Indian blood predominated in each of Dan and Ritter's children, so that they possessed a strong native dignity, high cheek bones, darkish complexions, prominent arched noses, and high intelligence. Each would have appeared perfectly at home on the Choctaw reservation in Oklahoma.

Dan's son LeRoy Wilson (known throughout his life simply as Wilson) was born in 1877 while Dan and his bride still lived on the King's Creek farm. He attended the primitive district school for a year, then entered the almost equally barren school that was taught at the mouth of School House Branch at Whitesburg. He was bright and learned quickly. After Dan finished his term as sheriff, he began to prosper in the law practice, and was able to send his son to Holbrook Academy at Knoxville. In 1897, at age twenty, Wilson graduated from Centre College with a baccalaureate in law. He was the youngest person ever admitted to the Kentucky State Bar. Licensed at eighteen, he had been practicing law two years before he graduated.

When Wilson was twenty and Dan forty-four, they formed a partnership for the practice of law—D.D. Fields and Son. By this time John C.C. Mayo and a small army of Roosevelts, Delanoes, Watsons, Flemings, Helliers, Camdens, Bradleys, Peppers, and other entrepreneurs were roaming eastern Kentucky to locate and buy the coal, oil, and gas deposits lying buried under the hills. Quite inevitably some of them turned to D.D. Fields and Son.

Father and Son prospered. They bought 45,000 acres of timber and coal for Swift Coal and Timber Company and even more for Mineral Development Company. They organized the Letcher County Coal Corporation and Caudill Coal Company. These and other corporate clients were involved in almost endless disputes over boundary lines and the legitimacy of titles, which were litigated in both state and federal court. Dan, the hill lawyer who never saw the inside of a college or high school except as a visitor, and whose license to practice was based on readings in a country law office, successfully defended his clients' claims before the Supreme Court of the United States. The directors of the land companies relied on this self-taught backwoodsman instead of graduates from prestigious law schools.

By his forties Wilson was able to retire and move to a new home in Lexington. He had two sons, LeRoy and Wallace. The former practiced law at Whitesburg for forty years and was county attorney for six of them. Wallace moved to Florida and, when he retired in 1978, was senior partner of the state's largest law firm, Carlton, Fields, Ward & Emmanuel, Smith & Cutler. At that time the firm had more than two hundred associate members.

After Ritter died, Uncle Dan, as he was called in his later years, acquired a young bride who bore him a daughter. Uncle Dan ordered a Ford tin lizzie and had it shipped to Norton, Virginia, where it was loaded on a huge wagon and hauled across the Pine Mountain to his home. There was a one-mile stretch of road passable to an automobile and each afternoon in dry weather he and his wife and baby went for a ride over the ruts, chug-holes, and rocks that marked the road. People were amazed by this audacious display of advanced technology. Dan died in 1927 at seventy-four.

Uncle Dan's first cousin, Ira Fields, never saw the inside of a school of any kind until he was twenty-three. The grandson of Isaac the patriarch, he grew up on King's Creek with Dan. He married Martha Raleigh and farmed near his father-in-law's place on the Cumberland River side of the Pine Mountain.

In 1887 Ira's five-year-old son Felix enrolled in the new school that had been built on Collier's Creek. James Lewis, who later would become a millionaire in coal, was hired to teach. The illiterate Ira also went to school. He was such a fast learner that in two terms he learned to read, work arithmetic problems, and write a fair hand. Ira then moved his family to Whitesburg where the boy continued in school and the father read law in every moment he could spare. Dressing himself for the occasion in store-bought clothes, he passed the bar examination in 1890 at age twenty-seven, three years after Jim Lewis taught him to read. He then borrowed money and went to the law department

of Centre College for a year. He had huge hands and a glib
tongue which he forthwith turned to politics. He was elected
county attorney from 1898 to 1902 and commonwealth attorney
for eighteen years after that.

Ira and his old pedagogue, Jim Lewis, organized the company
that brought the first telephone line to landlocked Letcher
County. They also chartered the county's first bank, which they
restructured as the First National.

Young Felix enjoyed a comparatively fine education. Ira put
him through Bryant and Stratton Business School (1903) and
then sent him to the University of Louisville's College of Law.
Like his father, Felix served a term as Letcher county attorney,
then was commonwealth attorney for two six-year terms. He
managed somehow to get a year of liberal arts education at
Valparaiso University in Indiana. His son, Emmett, told me
that this educational venture was undertaken simply "because
he wanted to know more history and to improve his English."
Emmett would also serve, like his father and his grandfather, as
counsel for the state. He held the office of commonwealth attorney for a total of twenty years between 1952 and 1974.

Porter Sims was for several years Kentucky's Chief Justice. A
man of great dignity and a fine lawyer, he gave the state's
highest tribunal a reputation for fairness that has not always
been a part of its history. When I appeared before him in 1954 to
argue for a certain motion, which he denied, he asked me
whether I had known the late Judge Monroe Fields. I replied
that, to use a mountain expression, I was "named after him"
because my parents admired him greatly. Judge Sims nodded
his approval. "Monroe Fields was the best judge I ever knew. He
would have made this country a great supreme court justice, and
I mean the United States Supreme Court in Washington."

Monroe was another descendant of Isaac, the pioneer. His
father married Joe Musselwhite's other daughter, Rachel, so
that he and Wilson were double first cousins. Born on those
rocky acres on King's Creek in 1881, he got his basic education
in the same school his cousins attended. Like Dan he obtained
enough knowledge to get a teacher's certificate. He taught
school four terms and saved every cent of his meager salary that

could be spared from life's absolute necessities. With that money and a modest loan from the bank his cousin Ira had cofounded with Jim Lewis, he made his way to the University of Louisville College of Law. In 1946, when Monroe gave me a letter of recommendation to the law school of the University of Kentucky, he reminisced about his own law school years. When he went to Louisville in 1903, he had one pair of shoes, two shirts, two suits of underwear, and three pairs of socks. He was without an overcoat or hat and his treasury was two hundred dollars. He was so poor that he knew he could never afford to return for a second year. The full course of studies had been extended to two nine-month terms and Monroe managed to sign up for *all* the courses by taking all the day courses and nearly all the evening courses. The dean opposed it, but young Fields stuck with the outlandish overload. During those nine months he made no trips home or anywhere else. He attended no ballgames or other entertainments. He worked as a laborer every hour he could spare from his studies. After paying his fees and rent, he had money for only the scantiest of rations, and subsisted mainly on potatoes, which he cooked in his room. And yet, said Judge Sims, he graduated at the top of his class!

When he returned to Letcher County in the spring of 1904, he was a pauper but had a license to practice law. He said that he had the "thinnest and shiniest suits in the world" and there were holes in his shoes. He began practicing law with the total commitment that is born of hunger. He began to win cases other lawyers had thought were hopeless. Florence Tyree, daughter of the town's most prominent man, thought well of him and they married. In 1909, when none of his cousins was running for the office, he was elected county attorney. From 1912 to 1924 he was the district's commonwealth attorney. Then he was elected circuit judge in a district composed of Pike and Letcher counties, a near miracle since Pike was twice as large as his home county and contained twice as many voters. He held that office for twenty-four years. Once he even defeated the fabled W.A. Daugherty and, in another race, was unopposed.

During his judgeship the Prohibition Act brought unprecedented violence to the Pike-Letcher district. Judge Fields said that at the beginning of one year, he faced a docket in Letcher

that bristled with twenty-six murder cases and the Pike docket
contained fifty more. For two consecutive years he tried nothing
but murder cases. Special judges came in between his terms to
try other kinds of actions.

Yet, according to Judge Sims, he had fewer reversals on appeals than any trial judge in the state. At one stretch he went
five years without a reversal. Later in his career six full years
passed without one of his opinions being overturned.

He was renowned as a stickler for absolute perfection. Orders
and judgments presented for his signature had to be couched in
sound grammar, correct spelling, and proper phrasing, or His
Honor would take out his pen and correct them as a school
teacher corrects a child's homework.

I never enjoyed the privilege of trying a case before Judge
Fields. He died of a heart attack in 1948, four months before I
was admitted to the bar.

The descendants of Isaac Fields held the offices of county
attorney, commonwealth attorney, and circuit judge for more
than a century. All were successful as lawyers, public officials,
businessmen and politicians. In a hard, backward region they
were progressive influences for strong courts, good roads, improved schools, and economic expansion. They were also men of
probity.

During my eight years as a professor of history at the University of Kentucky, I discussed this phenomenon of familial
strength and excellence with many colleagues, asking their
opinions about how and why these people had surmounted poverty and ignorance. One postulated that it was a result of the
example set by Isaac Fields. His support for the *principle* of
education had carried over to his descendants and had fired
their imaginations even after his death.

Another pointed to the marriages with the two Musselwhite
girls and spoke of a resulting hybrid vigor. He pointed to Alcy
Day, a close relative of John Day, the great Virginia and Tennessee frontiersman. "They began with strong stock and strengthened it in later years," he opined.

A third professor allowed that "it was a matter of the times."
In the same era people of unusual ability were breaking out of
the cultural and economic shells forged by the frontier experi-

ence. He felt that the Civil War started a cycle of scientific, technological, and financial expansion. "They were just part of the general upthrusting that characterized American society in post-Civil War decades."

Still another pointed to land exhaustion. In his view, "If they had grown up to a legacy of fertile soil, they would have remained content to farm. As it was, necessity forced them to turn to new ways of making a living. Some people starved out and left the country or became coal miners. The Fieldses stayed at home but adopted the law as a new means for survival."

Or perhaps, as is sometimes heard in the hills, it was all a matter of destiny—"the Lord's will."

As one listens to the explanations for poverty and failure that flow from sociological experts, inevitable questions arise: Why were these men not trapped in ignorance? Why did King's Creek not become a rural ghetto that held them fast in poverty and passivity? How could they have sought learning without being "counseled" to do so, and how could they have excelled without "remediation" to bring them abreast of more favored people elsewhere? Coming from such a poor and deprived community, why did they not become anti-social and turn to crime as a way of "venting their aggressiveness"? And what might have been their fate if they had been told as children that they were "disadvantaged," and offered today's wide range of public assistance and "guidance"?

Whatever the reason or reasons, these people did not submit to poverty and failure. As children, they never thought of themselves as disadvantaged but used whatever opportunities were available to them. Some opportunities they created, others they altered to fit their needs and circumstances. As one person became established, he helped the others. All contributed to the commonweal. To my mind, they provide the finest example of society operating at its best through individual effort.